S.K. RAPID (AUSTRIA)
WEDNESDAY, FEB. 26th
Kick-off 7-45 p.m.
Admission 6/6
№ 4951
ADULTS
CHAMPIONS LEAGUE
MATCH
MANCHESTER UNITED
BRUXELLES (Heysel)
BRUSSEL (Heizel)
INVITATION PERSONNELLE
PERSOONLIJKE UITNODIGING
SATURDAY, MARCH 18th
Admission 35p
№ 5648
TOTTENHAM HOTSPUR Football & Athletic Co. Ltd.
№ 10999
F.A. CUP, 3rd ROUND (REPLAY)
Tottenham Hotspur
v
MANCHESTER UNITED
AT WHITE HART LANE
On WEDNESDAY, 31st JAN., 1968
Kick-off 7.45 p.m.
5/-
GROUND TICKET
THIS PORTION TO BE RETAINED
G. W. JONES Secretary
FOOTBALL ASSOCIATION
CHALLENGE CUP
FINAL TIE
REPLAY
Thursday, 17th May 1990
Kick-Off 7.30 p.m.
LEEDS UNITED
SHEFFIELD WEDNESDAY
HILLSBOROUGH
FOOTBALL ASSOCIATION SEMI-FINAL
CHELSEA V MANCHESTER UNITED
SATURDAY 19 MAY 2018
KICK OFF 17:15
ENTRANCES OPEN 15:15
£ 70.00
FINAL
Fly Emirates
NOTHING IS CERTAIN
VILLARREAL CF vs MANCHESTER UNITED FC
GDANSK STADIUM
26 MAY 2021 21:00
GATES OPEN: 18:00
#UELfinal
European/Sth. American Cup
Final Tie—2nd Leg
MANCHESTER UNITED
v
ESTUDIANTES DE LA PLATA
WEDNESDAY, OCT. 16th
Kick-off 7-45 p.m.
Admission 12/6
PADDOCK
STRETFORD END
ADULTS
Enter by turnstiles 62—67
№ 3499
UNITED
v.
EVERTON
WEDNESDAY 1st DEC., 1976
Kick-off 7-30 p.m.
№ 5492
WANDERERS versus MANCHESTER UNITED
SATURDAY, 26th MARCH
SEMI-FINAL REPLAY
Monday, 23rd March, 197
MANCHESTER UNITED
versus
LEEDS UNITED
Kick-off 7-30 p.m.
EUROPA LEAGUE
UEFA.com
RESPECT
Zorya Luhansk
Manchester United Manchester
08.12.2016
20:00
The Football Association Challenge Cup Final Tie
SAT., 21 MAY, 1983
KICK-OFF 3.00 p.m.
TURNSTILES G
ENTRANCE 74
ROW 13
SEAT 95
THE EMPIRE STADIUM, WEMBLEY
The Football Association Challenge Cup Competition
FINAL TIE
SAT. MAY 21, 1977
KICK-OFF 3 p.m.
TURNSTILES F
ENTRANCE 76
ROW 24
SEAT 5
NORTH STAND SEAT
£5.00
TO BE RETAINED
SEE PLAN AND CONDITIONS ON BACK
CUP FINAL 1992
seat has been reserved for your use on
NUMBER 7 COACH
AC MILAN
UEFA Champi
Tues 24th April 2007 KO:7.45pm
ST Adult £49.00
Mr B Vincent
South Stand Upper
RUMBELOWS LEAGUE CUP FINAL
RUMBELOWS LEAGUE CUP
Sunday 21st April 1991
Kick Off is at 3.00 pm
FOR SEATING PURPOSE ONLY
39 3

MANCHESTER UNITED
SCRAPBOOK

Written By
Michael O'Neill

sona
BOOKS

sona BOOKS

First published by Danann Media Publishing Ltd 2017
This updated third edition published by Danann Media Publishing Ltd 2023

CAT NO: SON0492

Photography courtesy of The Press Association & Getty Images, Photoshot, UPPA, Talking Sport, Fotosports
Topical Press Agency
Getty Images; Michael Regan, Laurence Griffiths, Clive Brunskill, James Gill - Danehouse, PAUL ELLIS/POOL/AFP, MAJA HITIJ/POOL/AFP, VI Images, Ash Donelon/Manchester United, Gareth Copley, Alex Livesey - Danehouse, Stu Forste, Julian Finney, Glyn Kirk, Shaun Botterill, Jan Kruger, Matthew Peters

Alamy; Xinhua, parkerphotography, ITAR-TASS News Agency, Allstar Picture Library Ltd.

Book layout & design Darren Grice at **Ctrl-d**
Book design © Danann Media Publishing Limited
Copy Editor Juliette O'Neill
Proof Reader Cameron Thurlow

Made in EU.
ISBN: 978-1-912918-54-6

the CONTENTS

THE FOOTBALL LEAGUE

Clubs dedicated solely to the sport of football were formed regularly throughout the 18th century. The London Gymnastic Society was one of the first created in the 1850s. The first club to be referred to as a club was the *"Foot-Ball Club of Edinburgh"* in Scotland in the period 1821 to 1824. Great Leicestershire Cricket and Football Club existed in 1840. The staff of Guy's Hospital in London formed Guys Hospital Football Club in 1843 which claims to be the oldest known football club, whilst Sheffield Football Club founded in 1857, is the oldest club documented as not being affiliated to a school, university or other institution. The oldest club still playing association football is Cambridge University Association Football Club.

Soon, club names that are recognisable to fans today were appearing; Bolton Wanderers (1874), Aston Villa (1874), Queen's Park (1867), Sheffield Wednesday (1867); and of course there was a certain Newton Heath LYR Football Club which was formed by railway workers in 1878. What would they say today about the extraordinary club they started?

The time had come to try and make a set of rules that would be adhered to by all the clubs. In 1862, thirteen London clubs met and hammered out regulations to govern the sport. This led to the formation of the Football Association in 1863 to oversee regulations for the sport.

No history of football would be complete if the name of Ebenezer Cobb Morley was not mentioned. He was a central figure in bringing the Football Association into being. He was a player himself and a founding member of the Football Association. As captain of his team, the Barnes Club, he proposed a governing body for the sport and so the meeting of the thirteen London clubs came about. From 1863-1866 he was the FA's first secretary and from 1867-1874 its second president. He drafted the *"London Rules"* at his home in Barnes in London.

EBENEZER COBB MORLEY

ORIGINAL HANDWRITTEN RULES 1863

Meeting 24 Nov. 1863
Freemasons' Tavern

The minutes of the meeting held 17th Nov. were read and Confirmed

Letter from Mr. Steward
The Capt. of Football at Shrewsbury School
The Rev. J. C. Thring
Lt. H. C. Moore
Mr. Chambers
and " T. Bell
were read

The Secretary laid before the Meeting the rules which he had drawn up in pursuance of the resolutions passed at the previous meetings which were as follows

Another event must be mentioned here: the first official, international game between England and Scotland took place in November 1872 on the West of Scotland cricket ground in Partick, Scotland. 4,000 spectators watched a 0-0 draw although the Scots had a goal disallowed. The very first game had taken place on the 5th March 1870 at the Oval cricket ground in London.

Most of the men playing in the teams at the time were amateurs, although betting had long been a feature of the sport. On the 18th July 1885 it was finally decided that football could become a professional sport. But clubs were still setting their own fixture dates and the whole structure was chaotic. Now was the moment for another man to step into the limelight, Mr. William McGregor, a director of Aston villa Football Club and to make his mark on history.

It was the 2nd March 1888. McGregor wrote to the committees of several football clubs to propose that a league competition would guarantee a certain number of fixtures and bring some order into the confusion that then existed. In Anderson's Hotel in London on

FOOTBALL.

MEETING OF THE FOOTBALL ASSOCIATION.

As usual, the Freemasons' Tavern was the scene of the annual rendezvous of the members of the association, which took place on Wednesday last. Mr. E. C. Morley, the president, occupied the chair. Mr. C. W. Alcock (Wanderers) was elected secretary and treasurer in the place of Mr. R. G. Graham, and the following gentlemen were chosen on the committee:—Messrs. W. J. Dixon (Crusaders), R. W. Willis and R. G. Graham (Barnes), A. F. Kinnaird (Old Etonians), J. Kirkpatrick (Civil Service), W. J. Cutbill (Crystal Palace), W. Chesterman (Sheffield), Vere Wright (Newark), A. A. Padley (Lincoln), and C. L. Rothera (Nottingham). The principal subject for discussion was the question of handling the ball, and we are glad to state that the meeting resolved that in future "handling the ball under any pretence whatever" was prohibited. It was also decided that "in the event of no goal having fallen to either side at the lapse of half time, ends shall be changed." These are two very sensible rules, and in the event of the first one being strictly enforced, we shall see football carried on as it ought to be, and, as it always has been at one of our principal public schools, made a game of the feet, and free from those unscientific and brutal mauls. The Wanderers, Clapham Rovers, Barnes, Brixton, Harrow Pilgrims, Hampstead Heathens, N.N.'s, Upton Park, Amateur Athletic, Lincoln, Nottingham, and Newark Clubs all sent representatives to the meeting, whose discussions were conducted in the most amicable way.

FOOTBALL

THE FOOTBALL ASSOCIATION.

The adjourned annual meeting was held on Friday last, October 23, when the following officers were elected for the ensuing year:—A. Pember, Esq., president; James Turner, Esq., treasurer; E. C. Morley, Esq., honorary secretary; J. F. Alcock, Esq., E. Wawn, Esq., H. T. Steward, Esq., and William Cutbill, Esq., committeemen. Letters were read from the captains of different clubs in the country, who were unable to attend the meeting, and the times for the annual meeting and for notices of proposed alterations of rules respectively were altered from the month of September to November. The working of the rules during last season was found to have been upon the whole satisfactory, although several clubs expressed a lingering fondness for some favourite rule of their own which they had had to abandon for the sake of promoting the grand object of the association, "uniformity." Still it is probable that the rules of the association are far from perfection, and we hope that at the next annual meeting we shall have such suggestions brought forward as will leave little room for further improvement. With this object in view, we should recommend all football clubs, whether in town or country, to join the association.

SPORTING LIFE 1870

SPORTING LIFE 1864

WILLIAM MCGREGOR, REGARDED AS THE FOUNDER OF THE FOOTBALL LEAGUE

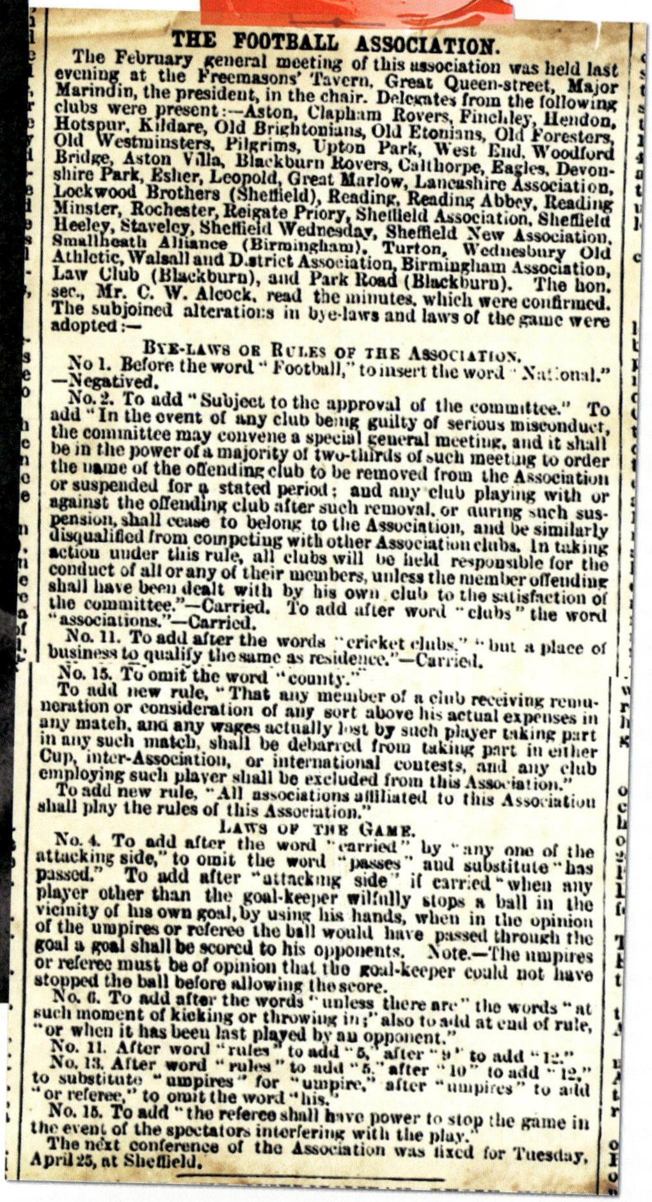

THE FOOTBALL ASSOCIATION.

The February general meeting of this association was held last evening at the Freemasons' Tavern, Great Queen-street, Major Marindin, the president, in the chair. Delegates from the following clubs were present:—Aston, Clapham Rovers, Finchley, Hendon, Hotspur, Kildare, Old Brightonians, Old Etonians, Old Foresters, Old Westminsters, Pilgrims, Upton Park, West End, Woodford Bridge, Aston Villa, Blackburn Rovers, Calthorpe, Eagles, Devonshire Park, Esher, Leopold, Great Marlow, Lancashire Association, Lockwood Brothers (Sheffield), Reading, Reading Abbey, Reading Minster, Rochester, Reigate Priory, Sheffield Association, Sheffield Heeley, Staveley, Sheffield Wednesday, Sheffield New Association, Smallheath Alliance (Birmingham), Turton, Wednesbury Old Athletic, Walsall and District Association, Birmingham Association, Law Club (Blackburn), and Park Road (Blackburn). The hon. sec., Mr. C. W. Alcock, read the minutes, which were confirmed. The subjoined alterations in bye-laws and laws of the game were adopted:—

BYE-LAWS OR RULES OF THE ASSOCIATION.

No 1. Before the word "Football," to insert the word "National."—Negatived.

No. 2. To add "Subject to the approval of the committee." To add "In the event of any club being guilty of serious misconduct, the committee may convene a special general meeting, and it shall be in the power of a majority of two-thirds of such meeting to order the name of the offending club to be removed from the Association or suspended for a stated period; and any club playing with or against the offending club after such removal, or during such suspension, shall cease to belong to the Association, and be similarly disqualified from competing with other Association clubs. In taking action under this rule, all clubs will be held responsible for the conduct of all or any of their members, unless the member offending shall have been dealt with by his own club to the satisfaction of the committee."—Carried. To add after word "clubs" the word "associations."—Carried.

No. 11. To add after the words "cricket clubs," "but a place of business to qualify the same as residence."—Carried.

No. 15. To omit the word "county."

To add new rule, "That any member of a club receiving remuneration or consideration of any sort above his actual expenses in any match, and any wages actually lost by such player taking part in any such match, shall be debarred from taking part in either Cup, inter-Association, or international contests, and any club employing such player shall be excluded from this Association."

To add new rule, "All associations affiliated to this Association shall play the rules of this Association."

LAWS OF THE GAME.

No. 4. To add after the word "carried" by "any one of the attacking side," to omit the word "passes" and substitute "has passed." To add after "attacking side" if carried "when any player other than the goal-keeper wilfully stops a ball in the vicinity of his own goal, by using his hands, when in the opinion of the umpires or referee the ball would have passed through the goal a goal shall be scored to his opponents. Note.—The umpires or referee must be of opinion that the goal-keeper could not have stopped the ball before allowing the score.

No. 6. To add after the words "unless there are" the words "at such moment of kicking or throwing in;" also to add at end of rule, "or when it has been last played by an opponent."

No. 11. After word "rules" to add "5," after "9" to add "12."

No. 13. After word "rules" to add "5," after "10" to add "12," to substitute "umpires" for "umpire," after "umpires" to add "or referee," to omit the word "his."

No. 15. To add "the referee shall have power to stop the game in the event of the spectators interfering with the play."

The next conference of the Association was fixed for Tuesday, April 25, at Sheffield.

SPORTING LIFE 1882

the 23rd March 1888, on the eve of the FA Cup Final, a meeting was held to discuss the proposal. Manchester was once again in the headlines when on the 17th April at the Royal Hotel, a final meeting created the Football League.

On the 8th September 1888, twelve clubs Accrington, Aston Villa, Blackburn Rovers, Derby County, Everton, Notts County, Preston North End, Stoke, FC., West Bromwich Albion and Wolverhampton Wanderers, sent their players out onto the turf for the first games in the new football league season.

Only once the season was underway was it decided that clubs would play against one another twice, once at home and once away, with two points awarded for a win and one for a draw. For the record, Preston won the first league title without losing a single game and won the FA Cup Final, too, the first league-FA Cup double.

Three clubs dominated during those first exciting years; Preston North End, Aston Villa and Sunderland; for fourteen seasons only three other clubs would win league titles; Everton, Sheffield United and Liverpool.

In 1892 the league expanded with the addition of a new Second Division. Liverpool, Arsenal and Newcastle United were now on the scene and a new name had been added to the First Division. A club with a glorious future had made its first steps to the top. Fourteen years had passed since they had first formed but now Newton Heath had arrived in the First Division.

Six years later, 1898, the number of clubs in each league had increased to eighteen and automatic promotion and relegation for two clubs was introduced the same year.

The Third Division was only added after WWI in 1921. By then another host of names that would later become legendary, including Tottenham Hotspur, Chelsea and Fulham, had been added to divisions that by 1905 had been boosted in numbers to 20 clubs in each. There were two third divisions in fact, the Third Division North and the Third Division South. Newton Heath by that time had become Manchester United having changed their name and moved to Old Trafford in 1902.

With the coming of WWII, the league was suspended for seven seasons. In 1950 there were 24 clubs in each of the two third divisions so there were now 92 league clubs. The third division clubs were amalgamated into a single division abolishing regionalisation and the Fourth Division was added in 1958. Four clubs could be promoted and relegated in the lower two divisions. In divisions one and two until 1974, two clubs made the climb or fell; the number was increased to three that same year.

The league now entered a period of calm with only minor changes such as altering the points system, three instead of two for a win introduced in 1981, and goal differences being taken into account. There was one enormous change ahead, however.

On May 27th 1992 the Premier League was formed. All First Division clubs resigned together from the Football League, which now operated with three divisions. The old system of interaction between the leagues, however, did not change but 104 years of tradition were over. The elite clubs were now, literally, in a league of their own. Money had tempted the top clubs and lucrative television rights deals beckoned them. The deal will soon be worth three billion pounds.

This wealth, of course, makes it almost impossible for a promoted club to compete with the big boys in the first season after promotion, and relegation often follows immediately. But the rewards for the successful are enormous with English Premier League clubs amongst the richest in the world and able to buy in players to make the....

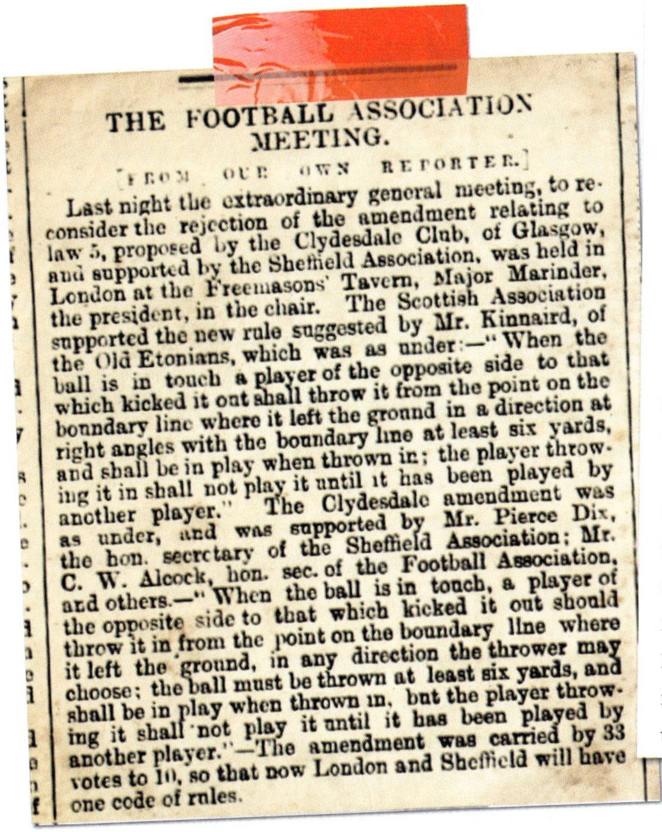

THE FOOTBALL ASSOCIATION MEETING.

[FROM OUR OWN REPORTER.]

Last night the extraordinary general meeting, to reconsider the rejection of the amendment relating to law 5, proposed by the Clydesdale Club, of Glasgow, and supported by the Sheffield Association, was held in London at the Freemasons' Tavern, Major Marinder, the president, in the chair. The Scottish Association supported the new rule suggested by Mr. Kinnaird, of the Old Etonians, which was as under:—"When the ball is in touch a player of the opposite side to that which kicked it out shall throw it from the point on the boundary line where it left the ground in a direction at right angles with the boundary line at least six yards, and shall be in play when thrown in; the player throwing it in shall not play it until it has been played by another player." The Clydesdale amendment was as under, and was supported by Mr. Pierce Dix, the hon. secretary of the Sheffield Association; Mr. C. W. Alcock, hon. sec. of the Football Association, and others.—"When the ball is in touch, a player of the opposite side to that which kicked it out should throw it in from the point on the boundary line where it left the ground, in any direction the thrower may choose; the ball must be thrown at least six yards, and shall be in play when thrown in, but the player throwing it shall not play it until it has been played by another player."—The amendment was carried by 33 votes to 10, so that now London and Sheffield will have one code of rules.

SHEFFIELD DAILY TELEGRAPH 1877

....TERRACES ON A SATURDAY AFTERNOON ONE OF THE MOST THRILLING PLACES TO BE.

IN THE

"FOR ME," SAID GARY NEVILLE, MANCHESTER UNITED'S CLUB CAPTAIN FOR FIVE YEARS, "IT'S HISTORY THAT SETS MANCHESTER UNITED APART FROM EVERY OTHER FOOTBALL CLUB."

The history of the club is indeed remarkable and the men who shaped it, football legends. But every fan, every player, every manager, owes the wonderful, turbulent years to one group of men; the railway workers from the Newton Heath Lancashire and Yorkshire Railway Football Club.

The Lancashire and Yorkshire Railway had been formed in 1847 and at the time football was still an amateur pastime. Many of the men in the workforce were keen fans of the game and by the mid 1860s, men in the coach-building section were already spending a few hard-earned pennies to play the game. It did not take long before there was talk of setting up a formal club. Frederick Attock was a superintendent engineer at the railway company and as a spokesman for the men at the carriage and wagon works he was the lynchpin helping to arrange money to set up a football club. Now, Manchester fans might like to skip this next sentence; Frederick Attock was a Liverpudlian. He approached the railway company's Dining Room Committee to ask for permission to play and also helped to get funds for the proposed team to pay for kit and equipment. The men would play on Saturday afternoons, the committee was told, mostly against teams of other railway workers. Permission was granted and Newton Heath LYR Football Club was on its way to glory.

WELL, NOT QUITE YET.

The team was just one of a whole number that were being formed at the time by working men everywhere in Britain. The initials LYR distinguished the team from a rival group that had been formed by the Motive Power Division, the Newton Heath Loco team. The Newton Heath name had been chosen because that was where the carriage and wagon works were sited and it was the town at one end of the railway line that ran from Newton Heath in Manchester to Leeds. Attock became the first president and with support from the committee, the team played its first match in 1878. Famous men were associated with the team even in those early days as Manchester East MP Arthur Balfour was an inaugural vice-president of the LYR team. He, of course, would become Prime Minister of Britain in 1902.

The club was based in Oldham Road at the Shears Hotel and their home ground was in North Road. It was just a field that the railway company had leased to them close to the railway yards and the lads had to be enterprising because it turned into a swamp in the winter months and became rock hard in the summer. But the new club was soon dubbed the "Heathens" and for the next fifteen years they

NEWTON HEATH TEAM 1892-93

gathered with their supporters at North Road.

Sadly there is no documentation to tell us what happened during those early matches. They would doubtless have been against other local clubs and surely the Newton Heath Loco's would have been the club's first deadly rivals! At that stage the matches would not have been part of an organised system. But the men were tough manual workers who were reported to be a powerful team determined to make their mark. They did. The LYR managers soon noted that the team was a good advertisement for the railway company.

With the growth in the number of teams came increased competition for the best players and Newton Heath LYR was in a good bargaining position. Players were known as 'shamateurs' in those days when the FA enforced the amateur status rule so money could not be used as an incentive. But because the LYR team was supported by the railway company, there might well be a good job in the railway yard available for a talented player willing to switch allegiances and run out onto the field for the LYR side.

In 1879 the team appeared in the colours adopted by the railway company, green and gold and for the next few years the team worked away building their skills and establishing themselves in the football world. At the end of their first season of 1878/79, public schoolboys the Old Etonians, won the FA Cup final. Even in those days, money could swing the pendulum. Nothing much more is known about the club during those first five years.

On the 20th November 1880, they played against Bolton Wanderers reserve team in their first recorded match. They crashed to a 6-0 defeat. A historic match took place on the 12th November 1881. Newton Heath played against West Gorton and won 3-0. Why historic? West Gorton later became Manchester City and Newton Heath, of course, Manchester United. Newton Heath is known to have played twenty-six friendly matches in the 1882/83 season.

FOOTBALL WAS STILL FINDING ITS FEET IN THE SPORTING WORLD AND SO WAS THE LYR TEAM.

BEGINNING

THE EARLY

The next step forward came during the 1883/84 season. The plethora of new clubs had led to the formation of regional club networks playing regularly against one another. Manchester was at the forefront of the organisation of these networks alongside many others in the north and midlands.

The LYR team had been playing against clubs from the Manchester district and in east Lancashire and in the 1883/84 season we find in the records that they took part in seventeen matches winning eight of them and drawing five. Only four defeats blotted their copybook. A creditable record. They were put in their place, however, when they decided to enter the Lancashire Cup for the first time.

The match against the Blackburn Olympic Reserves on the 27th October 1883 was the club's first match in an official competition. Although they were level shortly after half-time with the score standing at 2-2, the LYR lads probably then fell victim to their rivals' superior fitness. Blackburn Olympic, after all, had won the FA Cup the season before. They were one of the country's elite teams so LYR's performance until that point had been more than creditable. Their more experienced opponents then took over the game and slammed five more goals into the Newton Heath net before the final whistle. 7-2 the final score. These were the heights that the LYR lads now knew they had work towards. They did not shirk the job.

There was another competition with which the Heathens could test their skills against the best. This was the Challenge Cup or Manchester and District Senior Cup otherwise known as the Manchester Cup. The LYR team entered the following season, 1884/85. The Lancashire Cup was another washout for them that season as they only managed to get to the first round before being beaten by Baxenden.

So when the Manchester Cup matches began a few months later the omens were not good. Eccles was their first opponent. There was a replay; the Heathens got through. Then they faced Manchester FC and again won the day disposing of Dalton Hall Owens College in the semi-final. The final was played against Hurst FC and watched by three and a half thousand spectators; the Heathens failed in their attempt for cup glory by the margin of 3-0.

But how close they had come! And the consequences were enormous for the men. Realising that the team was a valuable asset, the railway managers began to allow the men to take time off work to train and prepare for games. The successful run in the Manchester Cup led to talk of the club becoming professional. So they entered the 1885/86 season with high hopes and firmly focused on the Manchester Cup. And this was to be the first of Manchester's glory days. Four knock out rounds took them to the final and along that route they thundered ten goals past Thornham in the third round. Before they entered the final at Whalley Range on the 3rd April 1886, they had also beaten Eccles 2-0, Gorton Villa 5-0 and Hurst 3-1. The Heathens' opponents that day were old rivals Manchester FC. Six thousand enthusiasts had turned up to watch. The strong wind that blew across the pitch favoured the Newton Heath team in the first half and they powered ahead. The half-time score was 2-0. The names of Black and Watkins were the first to begin the list of forwards that would score for the team in a cup final. There was some dispute about Watkins' goal, the claim being that he had handled the ball. The goal was allowed, however, and at the final whistle, Manchester FC trailed 2-1 and the Heathens had

1902-03 SQUAD

gained their first club trophy, the Manchester Cup.

Buoyed by this success, Newton Heath wanted to be part of the new wave of professionalism sweeping through the game and in the 1886/87 season they entered the FA Cup. They were also signing up talented players like Jack Powell who came to join them from Bolton Wanderers - and took up a job as a fitter at the railway company.

THERE WAS ANOTHER CONTROVERSY AROUND THE CORNER.

The Heathens met Fleetwood Rangers at Fleetwood Park in the first round of the FA Cup, so it was a duel between Lancastrians. Some two thousand people turned up to see their teams and after full time the score was 2-2. The referee asked if both sides would play extra time. Jack Powell, who was now captain of the Heathens, refused, whereupon the referee disqualified the team and awarded victory to Fleetwood.

Protestations to the FA proved futile so the club boycotted the competition for the next two years. Success also eluded them in the Manchester Cup that year. Newton Heath made it through to the final thrashing Gorton Villa 11-1 along the way, but lost 2-1 to West Manchester in the final.

In 1888 the Football League was founded and Newton Heath was anxious to join up; they were signing the best players they could from anywhere in the country. They had entered the year buoyed by victory in the Manchester Cup final in 1887 when they had beaten Denton 7-1 to gain their second trophy. Nonetheless, they were not judged to be a good enough team for the Football League being given just one vote for their application so they had to content themselves with becoming members of the Combination, a league of teams from the midlands and north of England. They only lost two matches of the twelve they played in the Combination. But without a properly organised central administration, the Combination turned into chaos and collapsed in 1889.

THIS WAS THE ALSO THE SEASON WHEN NEWTON HEATH CHANGED ITS COLOURS TO RED AND WHITE.

The Manchester Cup beckoned again and they set out with determination to succeed. Revenge against West Manchester came with a 2-1 win followed by Ardwick, 4-1, Manchester Welsh, 2-1 and then the final against Hooley Hill. They triumphed, 7-0 winners.

Yet there were big changes ahead for the team as they approached the final decade of the century. Denied entry to the Football League, Newton Heath helped in the formation of the Football Alliance for teams that had not yet ben able to secure a place the league. The team finished the season in eighth place out of twelve teams in the Alliance. They decided to re-enter the FA Cup but had the misfortune to face Preston North End,

YEARS

1905-06 SQUAD

"The Invincibles" and were soundly knocked out of the competition 6-1. The one ray of hope that year was the Manchester Cup, where they took the trophy once again, the third time, 5-2 winners against Royton.

A decision was finally taken to completely sever the connection with the railway company, a step that could not have been taken lightly as the company's money was guaranteed to the club, without it, existence was a risky business. The club changed its name to just Newton Heath, the LYR was gone. The results from the season were not encouraging either and after heavy defeats, 6-3 against Crewe Alexandra, 8-2 against Nottingham Forest, they were dangling on ninth position in the Alliance. They were knocked out of the FA Cup, the Lancashire Cup and the Manchester Cup although they only lost in the final to old rival West Manchester 1-0. Had it been a mistake to sever ties with the railway company?

Entering another season in the Alliance League, the Heathens were now a limited company. A. H. 'Alf' Albut ran the company with its £2,000 worth of shares and was also team manager. And the team itself? Suddenly the ball began to run in their favour and their skills began to show dividends, too. 10-1 winners over Lincoln City, 4-2 at Sheffield Wednesday, 5-0 against Walsall Town Swifts, 4-0 against Bootle. The results were so good that they finished the third season in the Alliance as runners up. Even the FA Cup proved less daunting. Ardwick fell victim to the newly-inspired Heathens losing 5-1 and the Newton Heath lads went on into the fourth round where they finally fell to Blackpool with a very respectable 4-3.

The Alliance League amalgamated with the Football League during the closed season and formed two divisions. Because of their improved form during the season the Newton Heath boys were elected into the Football League First Division. They had come a long way since 1878. Now they were amongst the elite of football.

The historic season of 1892/93 began. With its slim resources, the club was going to have to play thirty matches in its first season against teams that had far more experience. It was certainly not going to be an easy task. To get to the painful part first, they were last in the division when the season ended having gained 18 points, five points behind the next placed Accrington

Stanley. There were many defeats to deal with; they lost 5-1 to Sheffield Wednesday, 4-0 to Notts County, 5-0 to Sunderland and then 6-0 to Sunderland again at the return match away from home. But there was a blistering 10-1 victory over Wolverhampton Wanderers to boost their spirits and it was fortunate that the relegation rules had not been introduced at the time so they got another bite at the cherry. The rules provided for a "Test Match", the equivalent of a play-off in today's terminology, against the champions of the Second Division. That year it was Small Heath, which in later years became Birmingham City. The first match on the 22nd April was undecided at 1-1 so the anxiety had to continue until the 27th April. A thumping 5-1 victory ensured the Heathens' survival in their first season with the big boys.

Life in the Football League continued to prove difficult. Newton Heath could not avoid relegation at the end of their second year, being doomed by Liverpool to the Second Division making it the first club ever to be relegated. But there was a positive side, too, in that they were able to hone their skills with teams of equal ability instead of fighting for their lives.

For the next few seasons the team firmly established itself in the division and did well, finishing 3rd, 6th and then 2nd in the 1896/97 season. Second place meant a chance to get back into the First Division but the team failed in one of the two test matches, losing to Sunderland.

It was clear that an essential spark was missing that could propel the team back to the heights. There were internal problems, the demon drink played a part and even in those days there were complaints by the fans and the press that wages were too high. Fast forward one hundred years and watch history repeat itself.

A new century arrived with Newton Heath stuck in the Second Division seemingly doomed to repeat its pattern of high placings in a division that now had 18 teams, but missing the big promotion prize. They performed well enough at home but goals were becoming scarce. Off the field, financial disaster was looming with crowd attendances dropping and the Bank St. ground draining money. There were a plethora of team changes. Joe Cassidy their star forward had to be sold to try and bring in some money. The crisis would not go away. Despite another Manchester Cup win in 1901, bankruptcy was now just a question of time.

The lowest point in the club's history was reached in January 1902. The president of Newton Heath took the club to court for failure to pay him a debt of £240. With its debts totalling £2,670 the club was served a winding-up order after a creditor's meeting and the receiver was called

1911-12 SQUAD

in. The Bank Street ground was locked. It was an ignominious end to so many hopes. The club had made it through twenty-five years; now it was declared bankrupt. It was following in the footsteps of many clubs at the time and that could easily have been the end of the story of Newton Heath.

There is a legend at Manchester about what happened to restart the club on its journey to the top of the football world. One variation of it is this; team captain Harry Stafford had strapped a collecting box to his St. Bernard dog, Major. When Major wandered out of the club one evening, a friend of Manchester businessman John Henry Davies found the dog. When he got to know about the dog, Davies wanted to buy him for his daughter and sought out the owner. The meeting bore fruit but only after the club had gone bankrupt. Davies was the managing director of Manchester Breweries.

Stafford kept the team together and playing and with the help of Davies was able to raise £2,000 to appease the creditors. The game was back on for the Heathens. The team competed in all of its thirty matches and finished 15th. They were safely home for the next season.

An era was coming to an end. Control of the club had passed to Davies and the other investors. Newton Heath had played their last match. From now on the men would run onto the field in red shirts and white shorts and the fans would be supporting Manchester United Football Club. It was the 24th April 1902. An Italian businessman Louis Rocca had suggested the name. For the next fifty years he would be the club's scout.

That name was to bring sporting glory unmatched by any other English team. More league titles, more major cup trophies than any other club awaited them.

Davies injected his enthusiasm into the newly-named club and the men returned the favour by regaining their playing form, finishing fifth in the Second Division. They had even beaten First Division Liverpool in an FA Cup qualifying round. It was a humble beginning but a good one for the new team. But could they now improve and rise above that barrier that had kept Newton Heath from taking the champion's prize?

Ernst Mangnall had taken over as manager in 1903. He became another pivotal name in club history although his appointment was due to an unfortunate event and one that had sad consequences for captain Harry Stafford. Stafford and club secretary James West were suspended by the FA for alleged illegal payments to players. Stafford had saved the club from extinction yet he was never to play for Manchester United again.

Mangnall set about his task and tried out new combinations of players that brought a third place in the league in 1904. At last it began to look as though the dream might come true. New players were signed up; one of the key men that Mangnall found was Charlie Roberts, brought in from Grimsby town for £600. The football was exciting, the crowds stayed loyal, kept happy by a waterfall of 81 goals, more than many fans could remember seeing for some time. Only because they stumbled in April 1905 did they finish in third place instead of higher. Liverpool won the title.

The team was now a force to be reckoned with. Six consecutive wins in 1906 proved that this was a team to watch and their solid performance brought them second place in the title. Even with Bristol City four points above them, the longed for promotion was theirs. They were back in the First Division. And they had thrashed First Division Aston Villa in the FA Cup 5-1. Mangnall's magic was working and faster than anyone dared to have hoped.

New players gave United a comfortable eighth place at the end of their first foray into the First Division. But that was just the start. Mangnall was buying goal scorers like Billy Meredith, Sandy Turnbull and Jimmy Turnbull and his plan paid off handsomely. United surged to the head of the table to become league champions, 9 points ahead of Aston Villa. It was an incredible turn in the club's fortunes. They started the new season with five wins in six games. Unfortunately they could not sustain their form and injuries played their part so that in 1909 they fell back worryingly to 13th position. At least the fans could console themselves with another wonderful achievement; the club reached the FA Cup final and beat Bristol City 1-0.

Manchester can also claim to have been instrumental in getting the P. F. A., the Professional Footballers Association union, officially recognised. Wages and players rights were still inconsistent at the time. In a showdown with league club officials, who had declared that any player in the union would be suspended, the United players refused to play, on the eve of the new season. The authorities capitulated and players who had been banned were allowed back onto the pitch.

The years that followed promotion were a roller-coaster ride for the fans and the players of Manchester United. Another legend was born in 1910; the Old Trafford ground, then known as United Football ground, was opened on the 19th February with a game against Liverpool. 45,000 fans turned out to celebrate the new arrival. United ended 5th that year and squeezed into first place the following year one point ahead of Aston Villa with a dramatic 5-1 win against Birmingham.

But again the jinx struck that meant they would not follow up on past successes. The new season began well enough and then ended horribly with relegation even waving from the sidelines. Rescuing 5 points from the final six games gave them occupation of the 13th position and safety. It seemed that the strange pattern of good and bad performances could not be altered and when Mangnall unexpectedly left the team to join rival Manchester City in 1912, more bad news on the field was expected. Instead the Red Devils reached 4th place.

And the next season? 14th place in the wake of heavy defeats; 6-0, 6-1, 5-0. The gloss was becoming tarnished. Not only on the field. The spectre of financial insecurity had emerged once more. The Reds were being forced to sell their best players, which could only lead to disaster.

BILLY MEREDITH OF MANCHESTER UNITED IN ACTION DURING THE FIRST EVER FA CHARITY SHIELD MATCH AGAINST QUEENS PARK RANGERS

And then came something far worse. World War One. Of course, the fighting would be over by Christmas so the league season kicked off as usual on September 2nd. The new manager John 'Jack' Robson did nothing to reverse the club's fortunes and only a win against Chelsea saved the team from the Second Division by one point. And then a betting scandal cascaded over them. Sandy Turnbull, Enoch West and Arthur Whalley were suspended. United were 18th in the last FA league table of the pre-war years. The United footballers turned in their kits for rifles.

* * * *

The Great War had devastated England's youth and with it, of course, football. Sandy Turnbull had died in the trenches and the new Manchester United, although Jack Robson was still manager, did not field a line up that resembled the pre-war one. The decline continued, 12th place at the end of the season and 13th the next year. The ominous signs proved correct. By October of 1921 Jack Robson's dismal occupancy of the manager's seat came to an end and he was replaced with Scot Chapman from the Scottish League. It was too late to stop the train derailing. The club literally hit the bottom. 22nd in 1922.

This inter-war period was an unsettling time to be a United fan. The roller coaster continued. It seemed that elation and disappointment had to go hand in hand and the 20s began with disappointment. Now back in the Second Division for the first time in 16 years, they failed get back out for another two seasons. The Reds had to wait until 1925 to find second place and begin 1926 where they wanted to be. But whilst the team gave solid performances

2ND SEPTEMBER 1912: MANCHESTER UNITED CAPTAIN CHARLIE ROBERTS BEFORE THEIR MATCH AGAINST ARSENAL

they could not lift themselves into the upper echelons of the First Division as teams such as Aston Villa consistently did. Ninth place at the end of the first season was good, but they could not even get up to that position again before the end of the decade. 15th, 18th 12th; the team was middle of the table material.

John Davies, the man who had been Newton Heath's white knight and rescued the club from financial meltdown, had been ill for some time and died on the 24th October 1927 at the age of 63. He had helped steer the club to the heights; now others would have to take up the challenge.

The signs were not good. Herbert Bamlett had taken over as manager in 1927 and yet three years later there had been no improvement. And the Great Depression was beginning to erode attendance which was reduced by five thousand in one season alone. Then the seemingly inevitable happened. 12 lost games in succession, protests by supporters and Bamlett was sacked. This was by far one of the worse times in the Red Devils' history. United hit the bottom again. Just 3,969 fans turned out to witness the sad demise of their club. With Walter Crickmer in charge the club was facing its old foe: bankruptcy. Players' salaries could not be paid. And then as before, a man arrived to rescue the struggling team. Local garment manufacturer James W. Gibson had been told of United's dilemma by Stacey Lintott, a sports writer. Gibson stepped into the breach in return for directorship of the club. There was little immediate effect. There were too many players for a start and no true consistency in the constitution of the team. But the supporters began to return with hope in their hearts and from facing the nightmare of relegation to the Third Division, the team landed in twelfth place. Nonetheless, a new manager was appointed, Scott Duncan from Cowdenbeath in Scotland, a former Celtic and

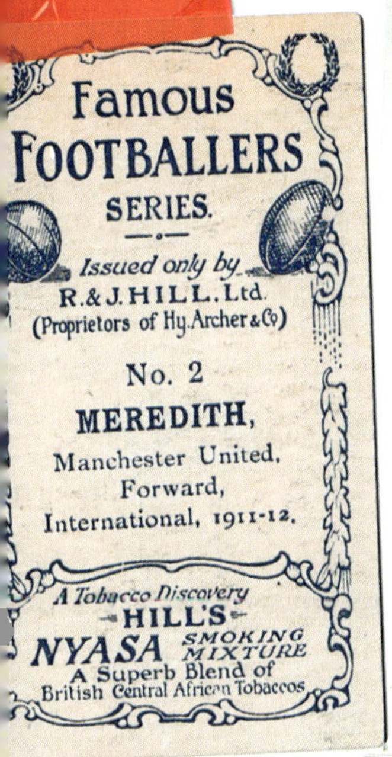

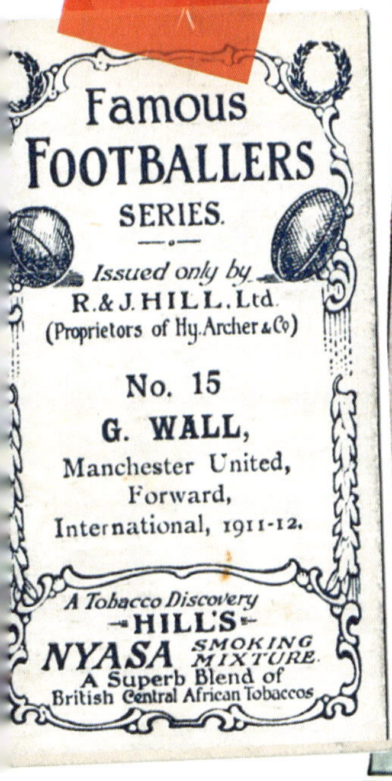

Rangers player. After initial wobbles, it seemed that the fresh blood in the team was working and United crept up to finish in 6th place. Forward Joe Spence moved on to Bradford at the end of the season, having created a record of 168 goals for his club and his record stood for decades to come.

Snakes and ladders might have come to mind when reviewing the United years before a new war broke out. Frustrating beyond belief when they crashed down to 20th place the following year, narrowly avoiding the drop. Then it was back up again to giddy heights with a 5th place in 1935, quickly forgotten when, with the defence not conceding one goal in 24 consecutive matches, United soared up to top position in 1936.

True to form, the red storm petered out almost immediately. Eight games gave them just three wins. What had happened to the wonderful goal-scorers of the previous season? And the defence? 78 goals conceded; the previous year it had been 43. The result was 21st place and relegation to Division Two.

Only to hurtle back to Division One in 1938 in second place. Although Scott Duncan had resigned, Walter Crickmer was back and there was a rising star to cheer the fans' hearts. Irishman Johnny Carey. Could he prevent the swift descent next season?

To everyone's relief, the Reds managed 14th place. Carey was impressive as an inside forward and when joined by another newcomer, John Hanlon, it was enough to keep United six points out of the danger zone.

Another era was ending as United's hopes rose. War was about to cut swathes through the men of the country for a second time that century. The season began with United playing three games beating Grimsby town 4-0, drawing with Chelsea 1-1 and losing to Charlton Athletic 2-0.

THEN THE GROUNDS FELL SILENT. UNTIL GERMAN BOMBS BADLY DAMAGED THE UNITED STADIUM IN 1941.

THE POST WAR YEARS & MUNICH

When the team regathered in 1945, full back Hubert Redwood had died of tuberculosis, Ben Carpenter of the reserves had died on the retreat from Dunkirk and youth team player George Curless died with Bomber Command.

No one knew it in the terrible emptiness at the end of the war in 1945, but there was momentous change in the air for Manchester United.

As clubs all over the country were slowly reassembled, United appointed a young Scottish physical training instructor to be the new team manager. He was still in the army when he got the job. He was demobilised in October by which time the FA had decided to stage an FA Cup as there was no league calendar. So the man to lead the team on the next stage of its journey, was Matt Busby.

The team fell in the second round to Preston North End 3-2. But that defeat, too, marked the end of an era, the era of snakes and ladders.

Old Trafford could not be used immediately because of the bomb damage so the team would play at Maine Road. The club was £15,000 in debt when Matt Busby and his assistant, Jimmy Murphy, set about building a new team using youth team players if possible. Busby resisted any interference from the club's directors, which was usual until then in football clubs, chose the players to be signed and took training sessions. United players responded to Busby's tough style immediately and the results were impressive. The Reds lost just one home game, and the title by one point to Liverpool who beat them at Anfield 1-0. A season to be proud of but the fans had been there before. What was in store for them? Second place the following season was the answer and it seemed the evil spell had been broken. The fans certainly believed so and returned in droves. Almost 82,000 watched the Red Devils play Arsenal, and Busby's

MANCHESTER UNITED GOALKEEPER CROMPTON RUNS OUT TO WATCH HIS LEFT HALF H COCKBURN (NO 6) CLEAR THE BALL NOVEMBER 1947

FANS BRAVE THE COLD WEATHER WATCHING ARSENAL AGAINST MANCHESTER UNITED 1946

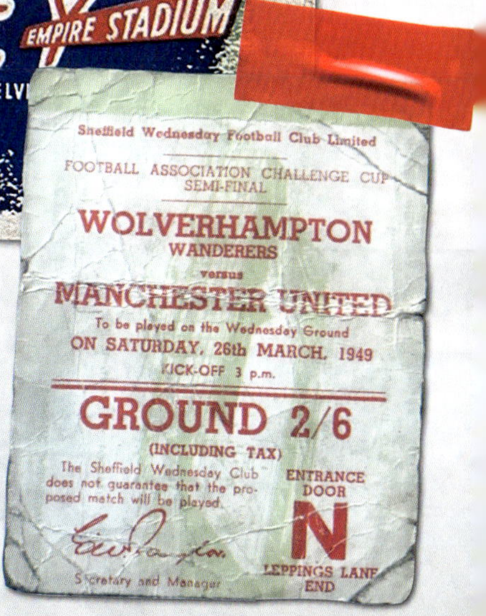

DISASTER

FA CUP FINAL AGAINST BLACKPOOL. THE WINNERS WALK DOWN THE STEPS AND ARE CONGRATULATED BY FANS, 24TH APRIL 1948

FA CUP FINAL AGAINST BLACKPOOL. JACK ROWLEY CHALLENGES HAYWARD, THE BLACKPOOL CENTRE HALF, 24TH APRIL 1948

CHARLTON V MANCHESTER UNITED. DELANEY IS ALMOST HELD BY BARTRAM, CHARLTON GOALKEEPER, 5TH MARCH 1949

United were now producing consistently good football and the proof that Busby's methods were the right ones can seen by looking at the league tables for the next years. Whilst the names at the top changed every single year (until United were at last on the top of the pile themselves) United came second again in 1948/49 and 1950/51 and fourth in 1949/50.

Busby was building the champions of the future, with tactics designed to score goals and a tight defence. The men did not disappoint him in their efforts but the Scot wanted more than second place. Perhaps the increasing rigours of the Charity Shield and FA Cup games were taking their toll but United could not quite close the points gaps each season. Busby's tactics produced the goals; forwards Jack Rowley and Charlie Mitten were having excellent matches.

Financially, the reopening of Old Trafford on the 24th August 1949 was a Godsend, as the £5,000 per year rent for Maine Road could now be put to better use. The 3-0 win over Bolton Wanderers was also an auspicious beginning for the newly-rebuilt stadium.

Matt Busby's tough attitudes were partly connected to another session of unrest at Manchester. Busby refused to follow the lead of other clubs and reward players with unofficial remunerations, so the disparity with other clubs began to claim heads. Charlie Mitten's answer was to move to Colombia and collect vast wages there. There were transfers of malcontents and Busby continued to press forward his system of bringing in young players.

And Busby's football was exciting to watch. United were praised again and again for their attacking style and when they beat Tottenham Hotspur 2-1, the fans were licking their lips in anticipation of a 1951 title. Tottenham got to the top four points clear of United. There was frustration, but at least it was at the right end of the table! And Busby was not a man to overreact. It would surely happen sooner rather than later. The foundations had been firmly laid and the way forward set out. Now everyone needed to keep their heads.

The new season of 1951/52 was a three-way fight between United, Portsmouth and Arsenal. Nervousness seemed to take hold as the vital last months of the season arrived. At this crucial time, Busby showed what a remarkable character he really was. He took the risk of making a vital change in the team. The new young full back Roger Byrne, one of the new generation of Busby men, was given his chance. He was strong, speedy, had great ball control and swept forward to press in attacks. Busby took him from the back and made him a winger. Byrne put in six goals for United in the next four games. Chelsea went down 3-0 and Arsenal collapsed

CHELSEA V MANCHESTER UNITED. GOALKEEPER ALLEN MAKES A DESPERATE DIVE, 5TH MARCH 1949

FULHAM V MANCHESTER UNITED. FULHAM'S GOALKEEPER, SHOOTS OUT HANDS READY, 16TH DECEMBER 1950

ARSENAL V MANCHESTER UNITED, CLIFF HOLTON'S HEADER IS CLEARED BY CROMPTON, 8TH DECEMBER 1951

before the onslaught 6-1. It was the final game and United had made it back to the top as champions of the league. It had been a wonderful season and Tom Jackson, in the Manchester Evening News, coined the phrase "Busby's Babes" referring to Byrne and his young team mates whom Busby was nurturing.

WHERE COULD THE YOUNG GODS NOT GO THE NEXT SEASON?

THEY SLID DOWN THE LEAGUE.

It was a confused year. Busby scouted for new youngsters and gave outings to 30 players to try and regain momentum. United won the Charity Shield against Newcastle United 4-2. The team played exhibition matches in America, which was good for club finances. Perhaps it was too much. The FA Cup saw them fall to Everton 2-1, and in the league the defence had become leaky and the goals refused to come either, so after being walloped by Middlesborough 5-0, eighth position at the end of the season was as favourable a place as could be expected.

When Johnny Carey brought his career at United to a close at the end of the season, it signalled the end of an era, too, the end of a link with the pre-war world. Carey was thirty-four and had made 344 first team appearances. Roger Byrne became the captain. The era of Busby's Babes was truly dawning because a whole raft of older players would depart the following season. Rowley, Pearson, Chilton and Aston who retired age 32. Busby was going for broke with his young players.

The new young team, led by its dynamic 24-year-old captain, could not get into its stride in the new season of 1953/54. Busby altered the combinations of players again and the team had to take painful lessons from more experienced teams. Gradually, the boys began to gel, playing the kind of high-octane game with sparkling displays of attacking football that Busby was known for and victories buoyed them. Lack of experience would let them down occasionally, the 5-1 defeat by Bolton Wanderers at home was one of those matches. But the lads made their mark and brought in a fourth place in the league and a fifth the next year.

The Club's league positions were encouraging for Busby and showed that he was on the right track but it was also obvious that the team was lacking the sharpness required for a place at the top. Yet with players so young yet able to hold their own in the table, the future would surely be bright. Busby kept his nerve; despite criticism from those impatient for glory and the youngsters often frustrating, inconsistent form. What happened next proved beyond doubt that Busby's Babes would be a force to be reckoned with.

In 1955, the average age of the team Busby fielded was just 22, which made even 26-year-old Roger Byrne look like a veteran. Everyone expected more experimentation and, indeed, a 19-year-old Eddie Coleman made his debut at half-back in November. The youngsters were able to challenge the teams fighting for the top place so nothing seemed to have changed, with the usual pattern of defeats and victories as the Reds headed into the run in for the end of the season.

Then, suddenly, the ball stuck to their feet. They powered through the final fourteen games and left the competition trailing in their wake with ten wins and four draws to finish league champions by the greatest margin of the 20th century so far. Eleven points clear of Blackpool.

Busby had in effect been creating his own training school for United players. They would enter the team already versed in his training methods and cast iron team spirit. Roger Byrne perhaps summed up one of the secrets that gave this system and therefore the teams, a spark of magic. "Nearly all of us grew up together as boy footballers" he said, "and the Manchester United way is the only way we know." Busby was also creating a solid core of experienced players with eight of the first team XI running out for three-quarters of the matches.

And as United left the opposition behind them again for the second successive season in 1957, the United boys were playing golden football starting with 12 undefeated outings at the start of the season. The core of 14 players including a young 18-year-old who would become a club and football legend, Bobby Charlton, was also a powerhouse in Europe, the most spectacular win being that against Anderlecht of Belgium, 10-1. The semi-final was the pinnacle of their success that year but victory in a final could surely not be long in coming. The league title was United's with three games left to be played.

The Reds got off to a fine start in 1958,

FA CUP FINAL AGAINST ASTON VILLA. INJURED UNITED GOALKEEPER RAY WOOD AND ASTON VILLA'S PETER MCPARLAND, 4TH MAY 1957

dispatching the first three teams they met with only one goal conceded. From that point on they began to falter slightly, losing 7 matches before the end of the year, which was one more than during the entire previous season. There was no reason for Busby to panic, however, as the lads whipped five goals past Arsenal at Highbury and beat Red Star Belgrade in the European Cup quarter-final 2-1. The team set out for Belgrade and the return match in January with high hopes of a semi-final place. Which is exactly what they achieved after a hard-fought match in which the Busby Babes smacked in three goals to lead 3-0, only to be pushed back, conceding three...

...THE DRAW WAS ENOUGH. THEY WERE THROUGH TO THE SEMI-FINALS IN EUROPE AND THEY SET OUT FOR HOME THE NEXT DAY IN GOOD SPIRITS.

Daily Mail man in the plane tells of disaster that killed half Manchester United team

7 BUSBY BOYS DIE

THE TEAM PICTURE BEFORE THE MUNICH AIR CRASH, 8TH FEBRUARY 1958

4am: Hope is fading for Matt

THE PLANE STOPPED IN MUNICH TO REFUEL AND AT 14:19 THE PLANE WAS GIVEN CLEARANCE FOR TAKE OFF FROM THE TOWER WITH THE TIME LIMIT EXPIRING AT 14:31....

...Captain Thain handed over control of the plane to his co-pilot Captain Rayment and the take off began. Captain Thain then noticed the port boost pressure gauge fluctuating with the plane reaching full power. Also, the engine sounded odd while accelerating, so he aborted the attempt.

The plane went back to starting position and began a second attempt three minutes later. Within forty seconds this, too, had to be aborted. The explanation given was that an over-rich fuel mixture was causing the engines to over-accelerate, a common problem with the Airspeed Ambassador planes. All passengers were asked to disembark and they went to the lounge.

Snow began to fall heavily so it seemed that all flights would be cancelled. "All flights cancelled, flying tomorrow. Duncan" was the telegram that winger Duncan Edwards sent to his landlady in Manchester.

A winter day in Munich when the world was united in grief

Several team members moved to the rear of the plane thinking it to be a safer place.

The plane taxied off to its take-off position at 14:56. (2:56 PM) and was informed at 15:02 that permission to take-off would expire at 15:04. By 15:03 the pilots had decided that they would start the procedure and keep close watch on the instruments.

"Zulu Uniform rolling" radioed the tower as the plane moved forward. Soon slush was firing from beneath the tyres and at 98 miles per hour the engines began to surge again. The pilot throttled back a little before increasing the speed again.

She would never see him again.

The airport engineer, Bill Black, suggested that the plane would have to remain overnight in Munich as the method of opening the engine throttle more slowly had not proved effective. Thain wanted to keep to his schedule; his suggestion was to open the throttle even more slowly. That meant that the plane would only be at take-off velocity when it was further down the runway, but the runway was almost 1.2 miles in length and Thain believed that this would be more than enough. So with the snow falling the passengers left the lounge just fifteen minutes later and returned to their seats.

"This may be death but I am ready" was one remark that came from some of the less happy fliers.

The plane was moving at almost 135 miles per hour now, a speed at which it would no longer be safe to abort take-off. Thain looked at the airspeed indicator needle. Instead of showing an increase in speed it had dropped back to nearly 129 miles per hour and then to just over 120 miles per hour. The slush was holding them back.

Rayment shouted. "Christ, we won't make it!"

The plane skidded out of control from the end of the runway, crashed through a perimeter airport fence and across a road. Its port wing was torn away when it hit a house, where a family of six lived. No one was killed in the house even though it caught fire. The plane lost part of its tail and the left side of the

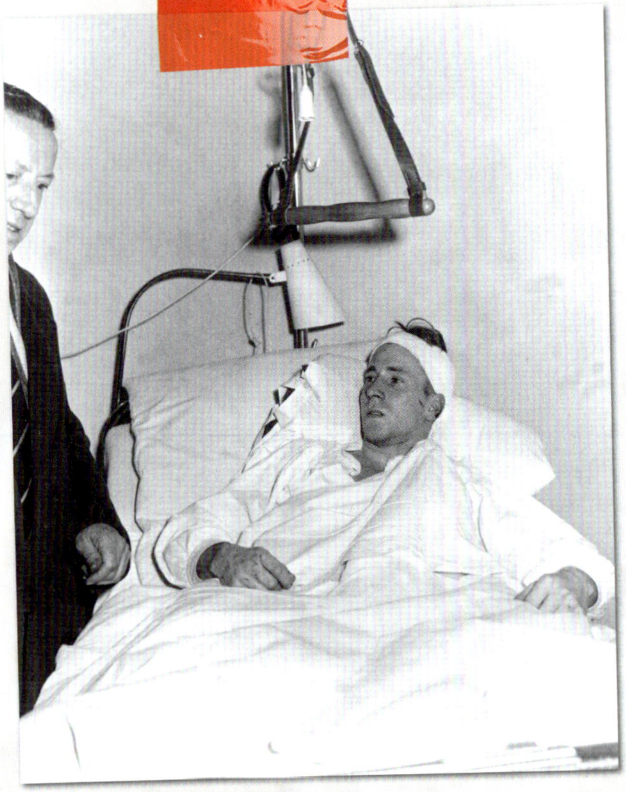

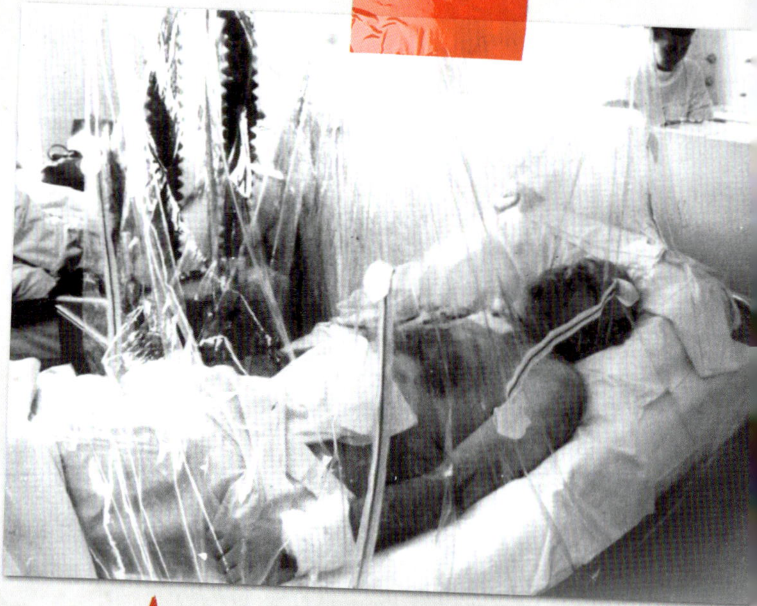

MATT BUSBY IN MUNICH HOSPITAL

BOBBY CHARLTON, SITTING UP IN HIS BED IN MUNICH HOSPITAL

THE FIRST PICTURE OF TEAM SINCE THE MUNICH AIR CRASH, 13TH MARCH 1958

cockpit hit a tree before the right side of the fuselage hit a wooden hut. A truck filled with tyres and fuel was parked in the hut. It exploded.

Twenty passengers died in the plane. The crash cut down eight players in the Manchester United team and almost cost them the life of their manager. The men who died were amongst the elite of British football; Geoff Bent, Roger Byrne, Eddie Coleman, Duncan Edwards, the greatest United player of his day who died of his terrible injuries 15 days later in hospital, Mark Jones, David Pegg, Tommy Taylor, Liam "Billy" Whelan.

The crash also took the lives of club secretary Walter Crickmer, trainer Tom Curry and chief coach Bert Whalley as well as eight journalists including Tom Jackson who had coined the term "Busby's Babes".

John Berry and Jackie Blanchflower came away from the crash with such severe injuries that their careers were over and they never played again. Bobby Charlton spent one week in hospital and was the first survivor to be released. Matt Busby also received severe injuries. He spent two months in hospital and was twice given the last rites. He almost gave up any thoughts of returning to the game; his wife gave him vital encouragement saying the lads would have wanted him to carry on.

Manchester and indeed England was in shock. Yet the matches had to go on somehow. Most of the survivors could not return to play. Goalkeeper Harry Gregg and defender Bill Foulkes had emerged from the plane uninjured and together with assistant trainer Jimmy Murphy they would "keep the flag flying" as Busby had asked them to do from his hospital bed.

The tragedy sat deeply in every heart. Crowds lined the streets as the coffins were brought home to Manchester. Thirteen days after the crash, with reserves and new signings, Manchester ran out into an FA Cup tie against Sheffield Wednesday in front of the Old Trafford crowd.

This terrible scar would take years to fade. The miracle was that United managed to go on fighting on the field in memory of the lost generation, and with a few of the survivors returning before the season finished, Bobby Charlton was one of them, the team reached ninth position. Busby was on the sidelines with walking sticks. Through the mourning, the club was beginning to rebuild.

It was never going to be an easy task. Yet six months after the crash it seemed as though it might be. Busby was back in full control and United were still playing the exciting football the manager wanted from them, and even though there was inconsistency in performance, a 12-game run without defeat brought hope....

…IT WAS ENOUGH TO SECURE SECOND PLACE, AN EXTRAORDINARY FEAT AND TESTIMONY TO BUSBY'S PERSISTENCE, HIS SYSTEM, HIS PLAYERS.

MATT BUSBY ON CRUTCHES, 18TH APRIL 1958 →

THE GLORIOUS 1960s

MAN UNITED'S MARK PEARSON (STANDING LEFT FOREGROUND) TAKES A SHOT, 10TH DECEMBER 1960

As the fifties that had began with so much hope and ended with such horror came to a close, the Manchester fans had to get used to another lean period with fluctuating fortunes.

As though they had been on an emotional tidal wave that had surged forward after Munich and then subsided, United were unable to gain traction in the 1959/60 season. One moment they were humbling the opposition, Leeds were disabled 6-0 at Old Trafford, the next they were being humbled themselves, defeated 5-1 by Tottenham. The forwards were firing in the goals at the same tempo as the previous year with Charlton and Dennis Viollet gathering 32 and 18 apiece in the league. The defence had become less sure of itself, though, letting opponents through to strike a goal 80 times. That proved to be the team's undoing and they sank down to 7th place and there was to be no FA Cup glory either when they were tipped out in the fifth round by Sheffield Wednesday by a single goal.

As before, Matt Busby's dreams would take time to realise, players were not made overnight and Busby was determined to bring on his youngsters despite less than perfect results. He needed his confidence because the mixture was to remain elusive for another three seasons. Busby was back in the position of needing to give chances to as many players as possible to get the right squad together and in 1960/61, a total of 27 players headed out onto the turf. Another name to watch had arrived, right half Nobby Stiles.

The team headed into the end of 1960 with two wins in nine games. With a 6-1 win over West Ham it was clear that the season was not for faint hearts as United walloped Chelsea 6-0 before conceding the same number of goals themselves. Bobby Charlton was still weaving his magic but attendances dropped as the team landed back in seventh position. Although Busby was unshakable in his belief that he had the formula right, it seemed that it was no longer working on the field. What was the solution? Buy more players to provide experience or stay with the youngsters and allow them to gain experience? The answer was to buy some and interchange 23 players over the season. Result? Ten matches without a win and eight goals scored with 31 taken out of their own net. The players rarely found themselves with the same team mates as in the previous match and United performances suffered. They settled despondently on 15th place.

IT WAS THE WORST OF TIMES . . . IT WAS THE BEST OF TIMES.

Busby knew he had to act before it was too late so he signed Denis Law for £115,000 which was an enormous gamble considering the club's finances and Paddy Crerand joined him from Celtic in February 1963 to strengthen the midfield. 10 matches lost before Christmas had set alarm bells ringing. Good FA Cup results were overshadowed by the awful league results that sent United hurtling down the table and brought the Second Division uncomfortably within sight. The unthinkable was now a terrifying possibility. There were four games in which to save themselves and the Reds lost one to Birmingham. Luck was with them, however, and it was Birmingham City who failed to get away from the third relegation position. United had lost 20 games but remained in the First Division and FA Cup victory helped to end the season with a glimmer of hope. 3-1 against Leicester City. But the fright of near relegation sat in their bones and there was discontent in the dressing room. They could not know that six wonderful, exciting years were to follow.

Busby had not abandoned his Babes; one of the most famous of all arrived in 1963; George Best, a Belfast lad spotted by a scout when he was fifteen and who was to score 6 goals in his first season with the Red Devils. Charlton, Stiles, Law, Best; the essential elements were coming together and United's flowing attacks began to show results on the score board. Ipswich Town took the blows losing 7-2 as did Burnley with 5-1 and later Sunderland by the same score in

1963 THE FA CUP FINAL AT WEMBLEY STADIUM, HERD SCORES THE SECOND WHILE DENIS LAW THROWS UP HIS ARMS IN DELIGHT, 25TH MAY 1963

THE CUP WINNERS' ENJOY THE MOMENT, L-R PAT CRERAND, ALBERT QUIXALL AND DAVID HERD, 25TH MAY 1963

the FA Cup. United were doing well in the league but with two replays against Sunderland taking their toll, United lost to West Ham in the cup final 3-1 and then had to go to Portugal to play Sporting Lisbon in the European Cup. They were roundly beaten 5-0. But United were challenging for the league title with Dennis Law hammering 46 goals home in all the matches he played, 30 of those in the league.

Another Manchester United first took place on January 18th 1964. Law, Charlton and Best were on the field together for the first time. A legendary trio, the magic trinity was born. Injuries meant that this did not become a permanent treat for the fans but the triple threat had given notice and any team who ignored it would pay the price. But the title eluded United; they were second to Liverpool.

A memorial plaque had been unveiled on the 25th February that year by Matt Busby in a quiet ceremony at the Manchester ground. It bore the names of the men who had died and a simple inscription "In memory of the officials and players who lost their lives in the Munich Air Disaster 6th February 1958.

With confidence justified by the previous season, Busby made Best a regular team member and bought John Connelly for £60,000 adding goalkeeper Pat Dunne to the

INTER-CITIES FAIRS CUP SECOND LEG MATCH, IN BUDAPEST. ALBERT AND NOVAK OF FERENCVAROS PREPARE TO TAKE AN INDIRECT FREE KICK, 6TH JUNE 1965

team. He stood between the goalposts in September 1964 for the first time and having had a shaky start to the season, the Reds suddenly became unbeatable for the next 15 games. Tottenham, Aston Villa and Wolverhampton Wanderers all felt the sting of the United forwards who were putting the ball in the opposition net regularly. Seven times against Aston Villa. Dennis Law was on great form cracking in 39 goals that season . . . which would prove to be vital as the season came to a close. In Europe, 10 goals put paid to Borussia Dortmund and another seven were struck in Sweden against Djurgardens, but that seemed to take the fire out of United's game at home. Only one of the next eight games produced a win.

The excitement of the season was to come from the clashes between newly-promoted Leeds United and the Red Devils. Manchester began a cup run that took them all the way to the semi-final and a confrontation with Don Revie's side that boasted Billy Bremner and Jackie Charlton, Bobby's brother.

They met on the 27th March 1965 and it was one of the most awful matches ever played. The ground was muddy and Leeds had a reputation for being as George Best put it, "cynical", which was an understatement. Best was intentionally kicked in the calf by Bobby Collins of Leeds as he walked down the tunnel to the pitch and given a verbal warning of more to come. Nobby Stiles would give Collins a hard time on the field for hounding Best.

It was more of a fight in the mud than a game and the players physically attacked one another with punches before the whistle blew on a 0-0 draw. There was not much to look forward to in the replay. Suffice to say that in a game that

BEST & CHARLTON CELEBRATE AFTER UNITED BEAT BENFICA IN THE EUROPEAN CUP FINAL AT WEMBLEY STADIUM, 25TH MAY 1963

was vastly more exciting than the one before, Leeds grabbed the win in the 89th minute with a Bremner goal. In the melee after the match, the referee was knocked to the ground by a supporter. It was a bitter defeat.

Now Leeds were going for the double but United went seven games without defeat before they lost their final match to Aston Villa. The defeat was not enough to help Leeds. The Red Devils sat aloft in the league. United had squeaked ahead on goal difference. Law, Herd, Connelly and Charlton had done their job well. The European title escaped them again this year although they had made it through to the semi-final against Hungarians Ferencvaros, losing 2-1 in a playoff.

The season had been a hard one physically, injuries had taken their toll and the new year did not start off well. Busby was happy that he had built a team ready for the top trophies. But with results in the league see-sawing again, a 5-1 defeat by Fulham for example, the European Cup had to give the fans hope that last season was not a flash in the pan. The fans had to be stout-hearted, for the season was disappointing despite a scintillating win against Benfica of Portugal, a team which included the mesmerising Eusebio, in the European Cup. Despite being told to play a tight game, Best was on top form and was unstoppable and United were soon two up in Lisbon with Best scoring in the 6th and 12th minutes. United won 5-1. The match is still considered to be amongst the finest United performances of all time.

The European dream died in the semi-final to Partizan Belgrade and the FA Cup vanished when Everton beat them 1-0. 13 games in just over 6 weeks proved exhausting and with Best out with a knee injury, points were dropped in the league and a fourth place on goal difference above Chelsea was all there was to show for a difficult year's work.

Busby had apparently thought about retiring after the understandable disappointments even though he still had reasons to be confident. This was a team capable of the best football in the country that now contained three World Cup winners in Nobby Stiles, Bobby Charlton and John Connelly. Also, Alex Stepney had been added to the team as goalkeeper.

The first matches of the new 1966/67 season did not indicate that this was going to be a special one as the see-saw of wins and losses got the team off to a patchy start. Then the gears clicked and the next eleven games brought eleven successes including wins against their closest rivals Tottenham and Nottingham Forest in the new year. Being kicked out of the FA Cup was in fact a good thing because the team could concentrate on the league alone. With keeper Stepney keeping the ball out of the net 11 times in 20 matches he proved a vital element in the successes that followed. With George Best able to play in every game, which amounted to 45, 11 less than the grueling fixture list of the previous season, United did not lose

DENIS LAW 10TH SEPTEMBER 1966

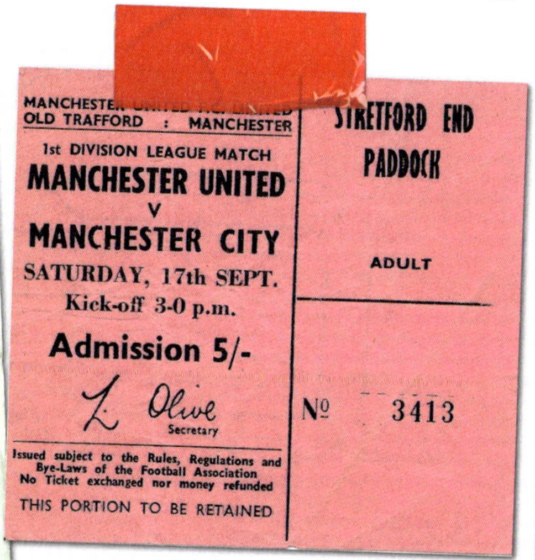

another game until the end of the season once the FA Cup challenge was over. Best scored ten times with Law again hitting 23 in the league and Charlton 12. Charlton was captain at United, one of the outstanding players of all time. With one game still to play, United outclassed West Ham, and sat unassailable at the top of the division. In fact, United scored so quickly in this match that Busby had not even taken his seat and missed the first goal. 3-0 up at half-time, he told the boys to keep it tight at 2-0. His team looked at him in astonishment and put him right, at which point he said the equivalent of go get 'em! United romped home, 6-1.

Who could have imagined that a team playing at the height of its form would not win another league title for 26 years? Not until the 1991/92 season would they again top the league. And less than one year after that, triumph legend Matt Busby would be dead.

Although the drought in the league had begun, there was glory to be found elsewhere and the team steered towards it the following season. They were a joy to watch and Busby was still bringing young players forward from the youth system to complement the experienced men. Brian Kidd and Francis Burns were two of the youngsters that season. The Reds got off to a good start despite a 3-1 failure against Everton and were even five points clear at the top of the table for a

GEORGE BEST IS PURSUED BY WEST HAM UNITED CAPTAIN BOBBY MOORE DURING THE MATCH AT UPTON PARK 8TH MAY 1967

MATT BUSBY HOLDS THE FIRST DIVISION CHAMPIONSHIP TROPHY ALOFT TO THE APPLAUD OF HIS TEAM AND THE CROWD, 13TH MAY 1967

period with rivals Manchester City on their heels. They surged into the quarter-finals of the European Cup. So all was well. Until February. The sparkle vanished, Tottenham put them out of the Cup and they lost five out of eight games in the league. That made the race to the top more exciting but uncertain.

With no other cup games, the European Cup was Busby's dream and in two legs, the Red Devils beat Górnik Zabrze 2-1 on aggregate in the quarter-final. Real Madrid would be their next opponents. The league began to slip from their grasp with two losses in three games the last just 4 days before the match with Real Madrid. So it was City that grabbed the league title two points clear of United.

But the stage was set for a classic United match, one of the greatest of all time. At home, Manchester had won 1-0 and that goal by George Best in the 37th minute was to prove vital, although few expected that the one goal would be enough when the Reds went to Madrid.

THE REDS PLAYED IN THE SPANISH CAPITAL ON MAY 25TH 1968.

United were playing a 4-4-2 formation and for half an hour the United defence held out the Spaniards and it seemed as though this was going to be a real problem for the Madrid side. The Spaniards were struggling. Nobby Stiles' marking was spot on but on the 32nd minute Amancio was able to slip from his grasp to take a free kick. Pirri was suddenly on the ball and United were one down. Now, good defensive play would no longer be enough.

From then on the game belonged to Madrid and they showed why they had become dominant on the continent.

Stiles was left trailing Amancio and ten minutes later the second goal had gone in. After almost twelve years as a Madrid player, Gento had hit the net after a mesmerising run.

United's hopes seemed to have been crushed. They were raised when Zoco managed to slice the ball into his own goal three minutes later. Those hopes were short-lived when the ball hit the United net for the

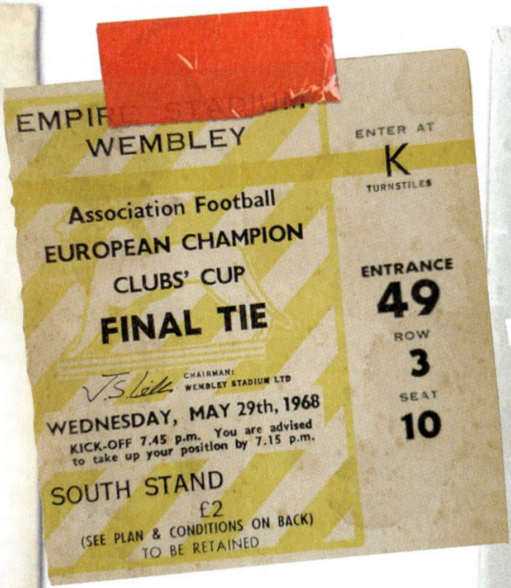

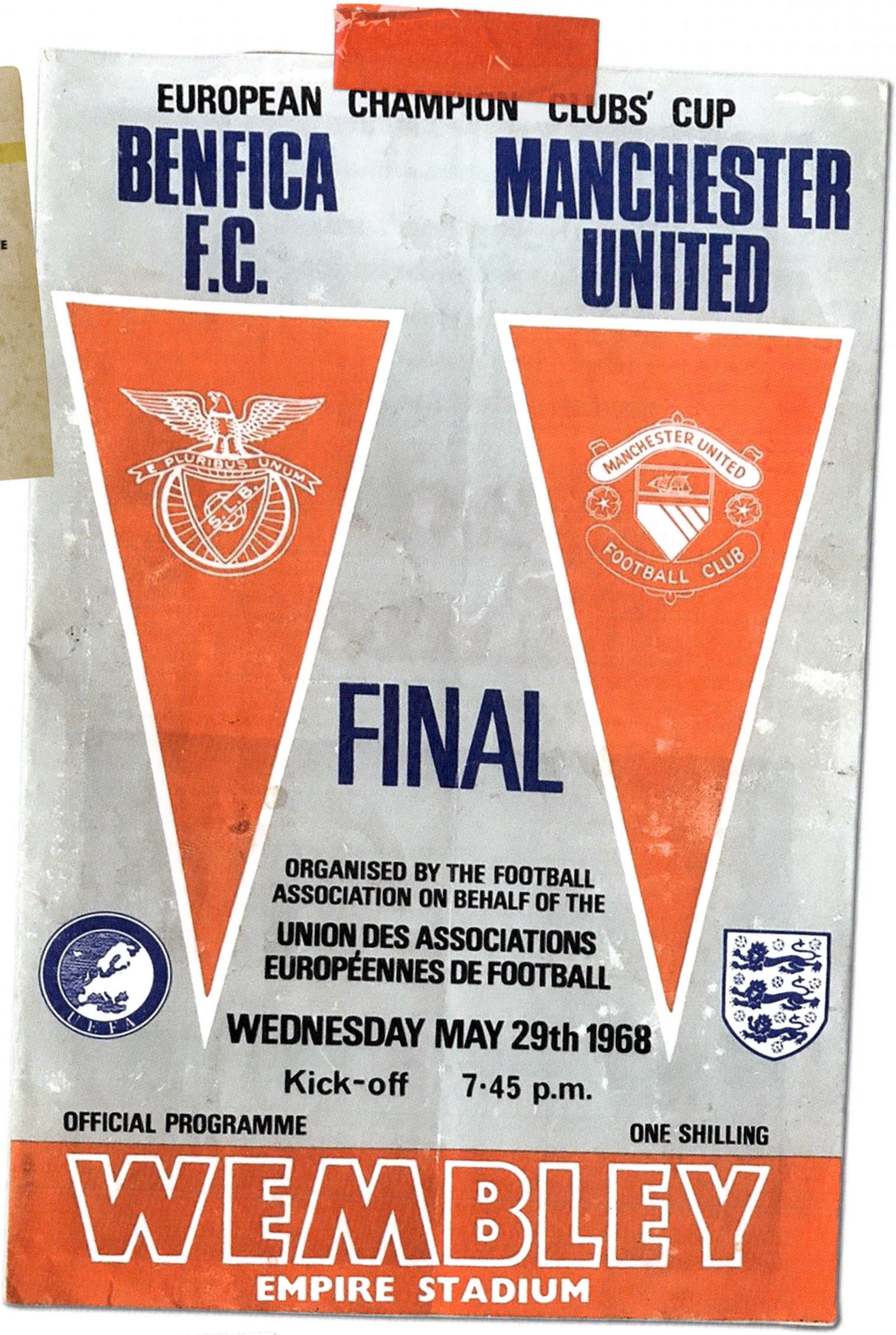

third time just three minutes later.

The fans were expecting a rout as the Spaniards took control in the second half too. But they had expended their energy too soon. They began to lose power and slowly but surely the Reds began to fight back.

When Sadler flicked a Best header in after 72 minutes, United were back with a chance. Now the Red Devils began to press forwards and Madrid could do nothing to stop George Best strike a perfect pass to Bill Foulkes, the man who survived the Munich Air Disaster, and he put United ahead on aggregate just 6 minutes after their second goal. Madrid had no answer and United were through to their first European Cup Final. It was a night of high emotion. Everyone was drained but jubilant.

Two weeks later the fans in Wembley Stadium were at fever pitch waiting to watch the team step out against Benfica. United were without Law, who was injured.

MATT BUSBY SHARES HIS JOY AND THE EUROPEAN CUP WITH PAT CRERAND AND GEORGE BEST, 30TH MAY 1968

IT WAS HOT AND HUMID IN LONDON. UNITED WORE BLUE.

The match was flat during the first half as both Best "El Beatle" and Eusebio the "Black Pearl" were tightly marked. And there were brutal tackles from both sides that did nothing to give either team the advantage. Eusebio managed to hit the bar once and then Bobby Charlton found himself clear. He rose up to a Sadler cross and put United in the lead.

Benfica did not break. They pressurised the United defence more and more and eventually with ten minutes to go, the Portuguese got their reward and drew level. There was a heart-stopping moment for United when Eusebio got through the defence. Stepney took the gamble of his life and decided that Eusebio would want a spectacular goal. He stayed on his feet as Eusebio fired the ball with all his might. It hit Stepney in the chest and away from danger.

In extra time, Benfica were still taking the game to United who were visibly tiring. Yet two minutes into extra time it was George Best's turn to break free. He did not waste his chance. He took Kidd's header, slipped past a tackle and, circling the keeper, slid the ball into the net. Now United began to take over. One minute later Kidd had made it 3-1. Finally, at 99 minutes, Bobby Charlton went up to meet a Kidd cross and United were 4-1 in front.

When the whistle went, the Reds were European Champions. Matt Busby had realised his dream of bringing the European Cup to Manchester. Some would say that the team was not as good as the one that had existed before the Munich crash. But they had brought home the European prize. There were tears of joy and it was fitting that the three survivors of the crash, Busby, Charlton and Foulkes were part of the magnificent success. Paddy Crerand recalled that all the players were looking for Matt Busby who was coming towards them doing a "half jog, half dance". He was then hugged by his team.

FOR MATT BUSBY, ACHIEVING EUROPEAN GLORY WAS THE PINNACLE OF HIS CAREER.

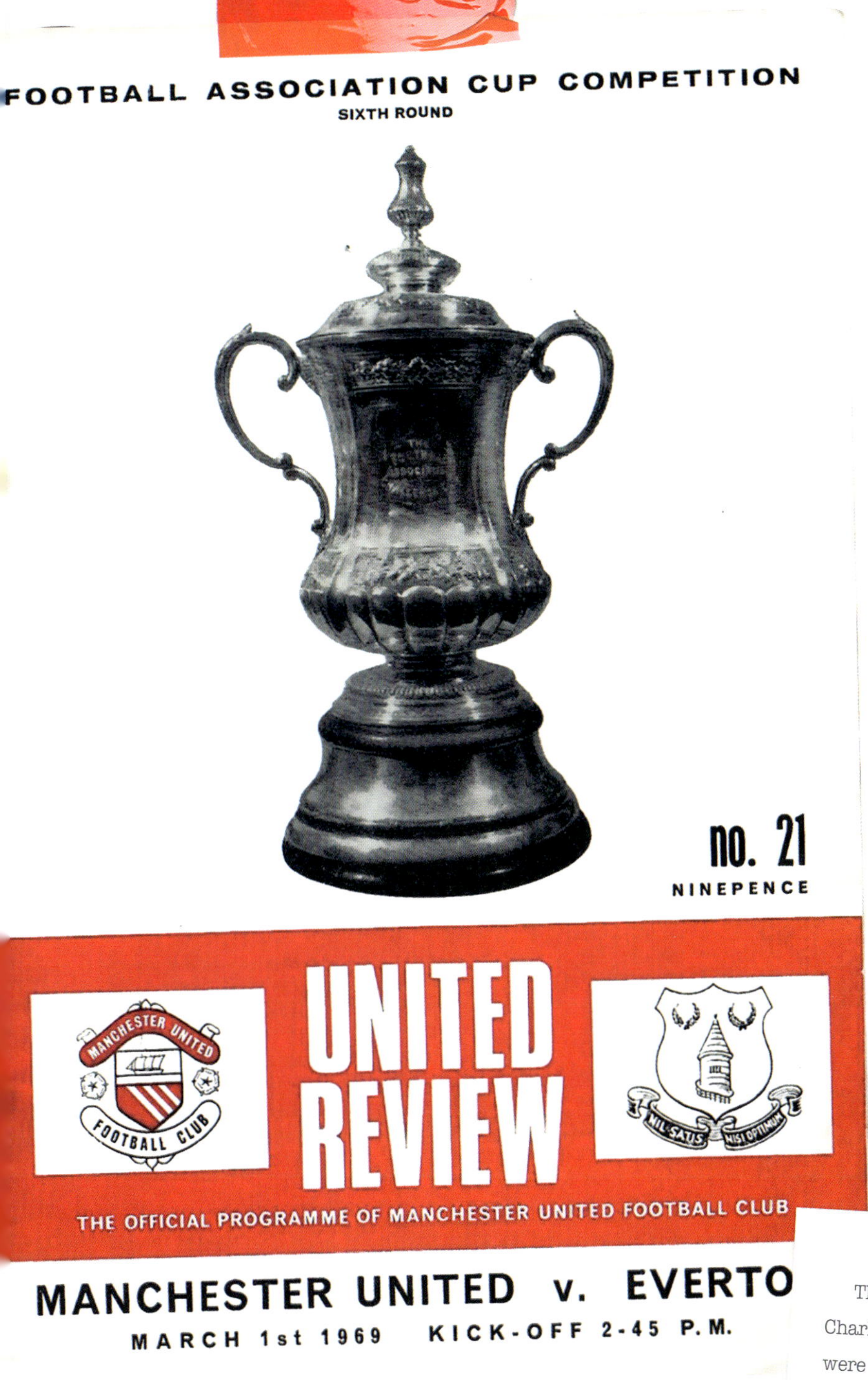

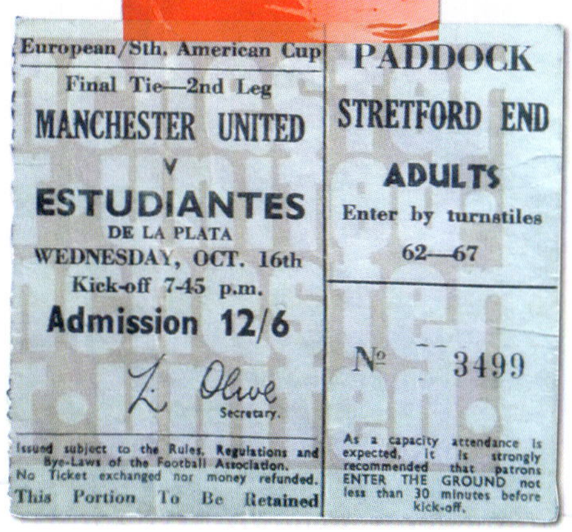

The team was in need of new blood as Law and Charlton were receiving more injuries and older players were taking part in less games.

The European Cup games in the 1968/69 season produced vicious matches against AC Milan who committed appalling fouls and United lost on aggregate. The top of the league moved further away, too, as their form stalled. Busby had become Sir Matt Busby but he felt that the time had arrived to let a younger man take over the reigns at United. This was to be his last season. So after 23 years, the career that had seen so many highlights ended rather limply with United in eleventh place in the table and no other trophies to compensate.

Wilf McGuinness was selected to take over from Matt Busby, chosen by the great man himself, who continued to work as general manager at the club.

McGuinness was 31 and well-liked by fans and team alike and had helped in Sir Alf Ramsey's 1966 World Cup success, but with the Manchester team in a state of flux, it was perhaps unfortunate timing for him. Busby had been a unique manager, it would take another unique personality to match his achievements.

Three points from six games was not a good start for the new "Head Coach", the title McGuinness was given. Ian Ure was signed from Arsenal and his presence was enough to stop the rot at the back so that the Reds reached the semi-final of the League Cup only to lose out to Manchester City and have the same thing happen in the FA Cup semi-final against Leeds. The old inconsistency had returned and eighth place was the final position in the league.

FAR BELOW EXPECTATIONS AS UNITED HEADED TOWARDS A NEW DECADE.

GEORGE BEST 15TH APRIL 1968

BOBBY CHARLTON 26TH AUGUST 1969

CHAMPIONS CUP COMP
UNITED REVIEW
OGRAMME OF MANCHESTER UNITED FOOT
E EUROPEAN CHAMPIONS CUP COMPETI
NINEPENCE
FIRST L
QUA
ESTER
TED
V
S.K. RAPID
VIENNA

Stadio di San Siro, 23 aprile, 1969
Prezzo: 150 lire
Old Trafford, Manchester, 14 maggio, 1969
Regno Unito.: 2 scellini
MILAN
1899
A.C.
MILAN
MANCHESTER
UNITED
EUROPEAN CUP
SEMI-FINAL
1969
San Siro Stadium, April 23rd, 1969
Price: 150 lire
Old Trafford, Manchester, May 14th, 1969
U.K. 2s.

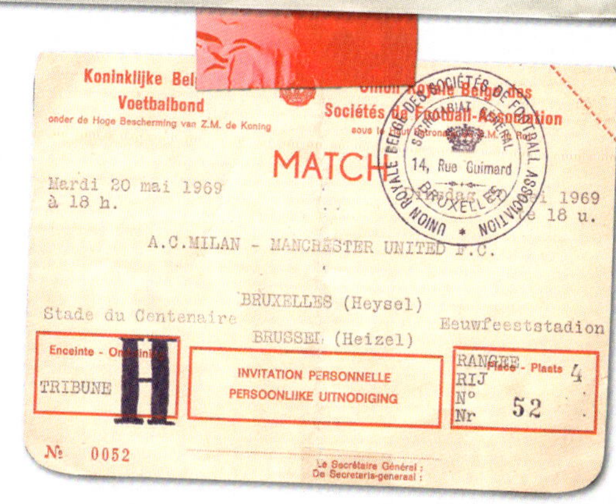
Voetbalbond
MATCH
Mardi 20 mai 1969
à 18 h.
14, Rue Guimard
A.C.MILAN - MANCHESTER UNITED F.C.
BRUXELLES (Heysel)
Stade du Centenaire
Eeuwfeeststadion
BRUSSEL (Heizel)
TRIBUNE
H
INVITATION PERSONNELLE
PERSOONLIJKE UITNODIGING
52
0052

FROM THE 70s

The first year of the 70's left United adrift on eighth place once more, Wilf McGuinness had been demoted rather than sacked and Busby finished the season as manager again. Change was certainly in the air. Nobby Stiles was transferred and George Best was unhappy. Early in the 70s both he and Bobby Charlton would end their United careers. Best's playboy lifestyle was causing both him and the club problems. Best failed to turn up for training on Christmas Day. He received one of many fines for disciplinary problems. He confessed to a drinking problem and even announced his retirement and although he played another 35 games for the club until 1974, he was an increasingly unhappy man. United's problems continued alongside their star player who wanted the captaincy and new players. Frank O'Farrell became the new manager for a short-lived reign in which United were eighth in the league for third successive season. It was an unhappy time and it showed in the results. The new season was even worse with United losing 2-1 to Bristol Rovers at Old Trafford in the League Cup. O'Farrell was not the man for United and he was fired in December 1972. The post-Busby era was proving extremely difficult to deal with but there was no time to idle. A new man was needed at the top.

The man chosen in haste was Tommy Docherty. As the Reds went hurtling down the league to 18th place only just escaping relegation, the choice did not seem inspired. Bobby Charlton retired after a record 758 appearances. United were a team uncertain about their future.

1974 finished what 1973 had promised. Docherty could not make his new team gel fast enough. Dennis Law was now playing for Manchester City, one of many of the old United squad who left for new teams. And Best.

TO THE

Wonderful George played his last game for the club on January 1st 1974. United reeled under the opposition blows and when Dennis Law struck against them in one of the last matches of the season, the death rattle was already sounding. United were relegated for the first time in almost 40 years. It is perhaps fitting that Charlton, Law

FERGUSON ERA

CLASSIC SHOT OF GEORGE BEST, 18TH SEPTEMBER 1971

MAN CITY V MAN UNITED, MIKE SUMMERBEE OF MANCHESTER CITY GEORGE BEST, BOBBY CHARLTON, 6TH NOVEMBER 1971

← MANCHESTER UNITED V LEEDS UNITED, FA CUP SEMI-FINAL AT VILLA PARK, 3RD JANUARY 1971

focus on... GEORGE BEST

FULL NAME: George Best
BIRTHPLACE: Belfast
BIRTHDATE: 22nd May, 1946
HEIGHT: 5 ft. 8½ in.
WEIGHT: 152 lb.
PREVIOUS CLUBS: None
CAR: 12-cylinder E-Type Jaguar
FAVOURITE PLAYER: The former Real Madrid star Alfredo Di Stefano
FAVOURITE OTHER TEAM: Spurs
MOST DIFFICULT OPPONENT: None
MOST MEMORABLE MATCH: Against Benfica in the Quarter Final of the 1965-66 European Cup. We won 5-1
BIGGEST THRILL: Every time I score
BIGGEST DISAPPOINTMENT: Not being able to play in World Cup Finals
BEST COUNTRY VISITED: U.S.A.
FAVOURITE FOOD: Chinese
MISCELLANEOUS LIKES: Reading, watching most sports, travelling
MISCELLANEOUS DISLIKES: Miserable people, delays at airports and railway stations
FAVOURITE T.V. SHOWS: Flip Wilson show, Marty Feldman show
FAVOURITE SINGERS: Tom Jones and Lulu
FAVOURITE ACTORS/ACTRESSES: Dustin Hoffman, Richard Harris, Steve McQueen, Rod Steiger, Catherine Ross and Julie Ege.
BEST FRIEND: My Bank Manager
BIGGEST INFLUENCE ON CAREER: Sir Matt Busby
BIGGEST DRAG IN SOCCER: Postponed games
INTERNATIONAL HONOURS: Apart from N. Ireland caps, none
PERSONAL AMBITION: To be happily married with kids
PROFESSIONAL AMBITION: To do well in the next World Cup
IF YOU WEREN'T A FOOTBALLER, WHAT DO YOU THINK YOU'D BE? I honestly don't know
WHAT PERSON IN THE WORLD WOULD YOU MOST LIKE TO MEET? Either Brigitte Bardot or Cassius Clay

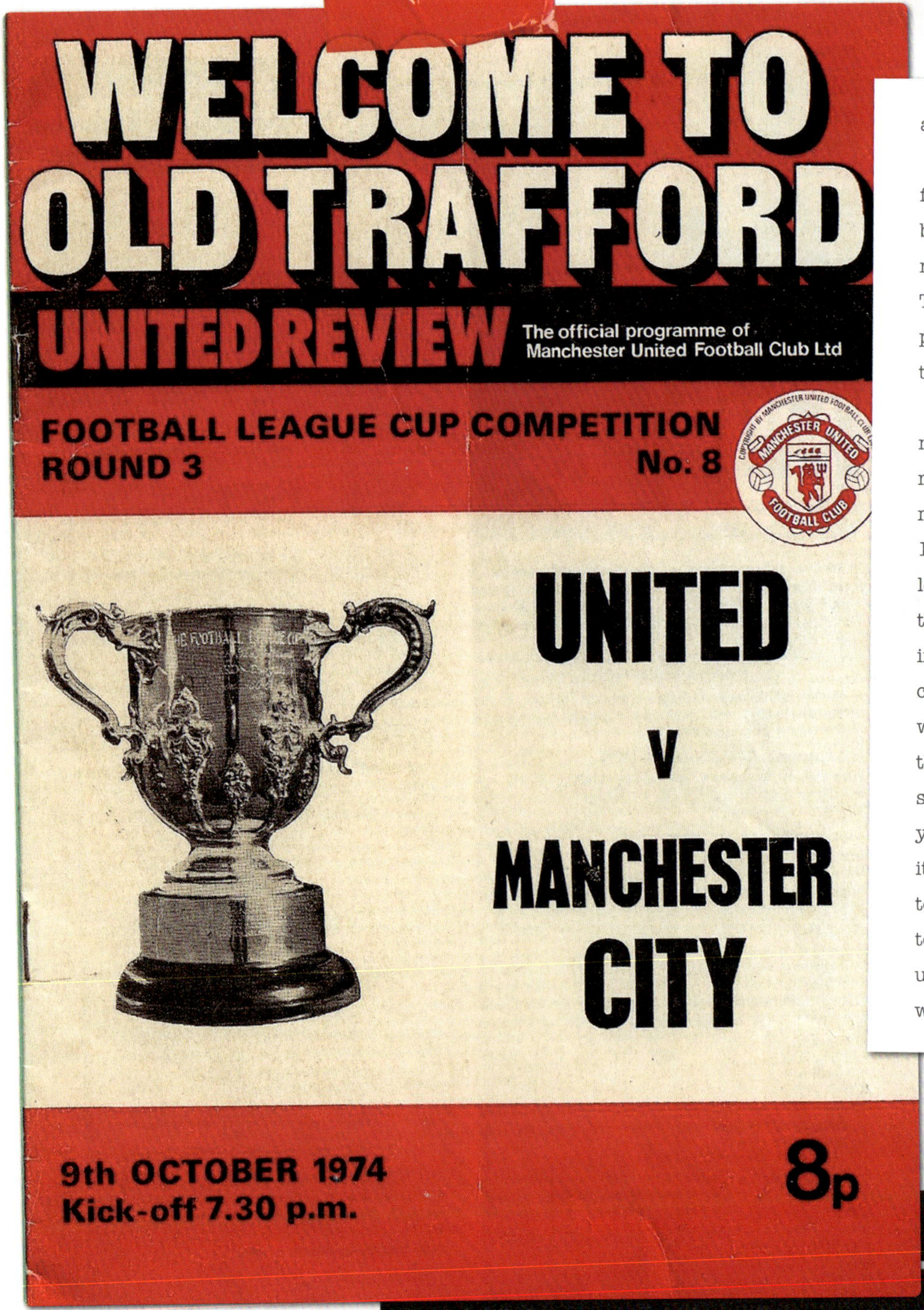
WELCOME TO OLD TRAFFORD

UNITED REVIEW

The official programme of Manchester United Football Club Ltd

FOOTBALL LEAGUE CUP COMPETITION
ROUND 3

No. 8

UNITED

V

MANCHESTER CITY

9th OCTOBER 1974
Kick-off 7.30 p.m.

8p

and Best were not in at the end.

But United were rewarded for keeping faith with Docherty when the team roared back into the First Division the very next season as Second Division winners. The cup games were disappointing but promotion was more important and the team deserved its success.

They were able to build on the success next season and a 14-game unbeaten run confirmed that they were a team to reckon with once more. A shock defeat 1-0 in the FA Cup Final to Southampton left the Reds without any honours at the end as they finished in third place in the league, but they had reason to be confident that at last they were back with a good man at the helm. So when they lifted the FA Cup in the 1976/77 season denying Liverpool the double that year, there was happiness all around and it seemed that the good times were here to stay. They slipped back in the league to 6th but that was nothing to the next unexpected shock. Docherty was sacked when he left his wife to live with the

MANCHESTER UNITED SQUAD, 1974-75

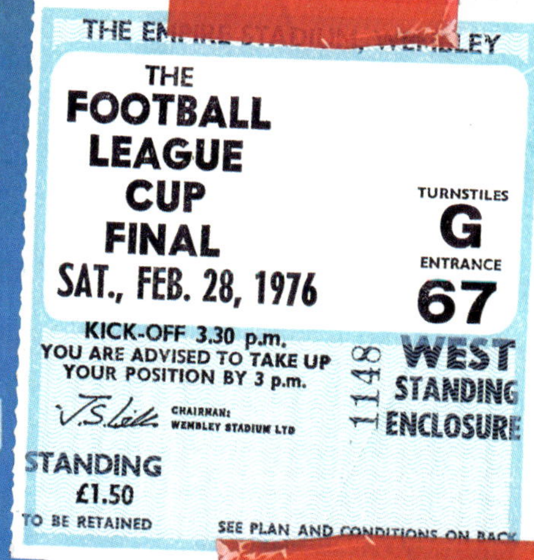

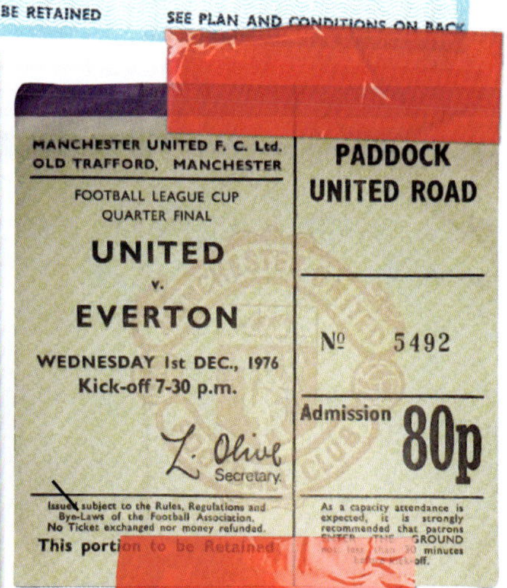

wife of the club's physiotherapist. The short-lived return to glory dissolved.

Another manager arrived, Dave Sexton, but he was never quite able to restore the shine to the United team. He began to dismantle Docherty's team and the results were not positive. Was this to be a repeat of life under O'Farrell? The FA Cup, the Cup-Winners' Cup, The League Cup and the Charity Shield all vanished from sight and tenth was an uncomfortable place to end for the 1977/78 season.

Nothing could be improved by the following year although there were signs of hope when the Reds reached the FA Cup final. It was a thrilling match with Arsenal ahead 2-0 by the 85th minute. United were able to snatch a scrambled goal followed by another almost immediately. But the Reds could not keep the momentum in extra time and it was Arsenal who pushed in the winning goal to win 2-3.

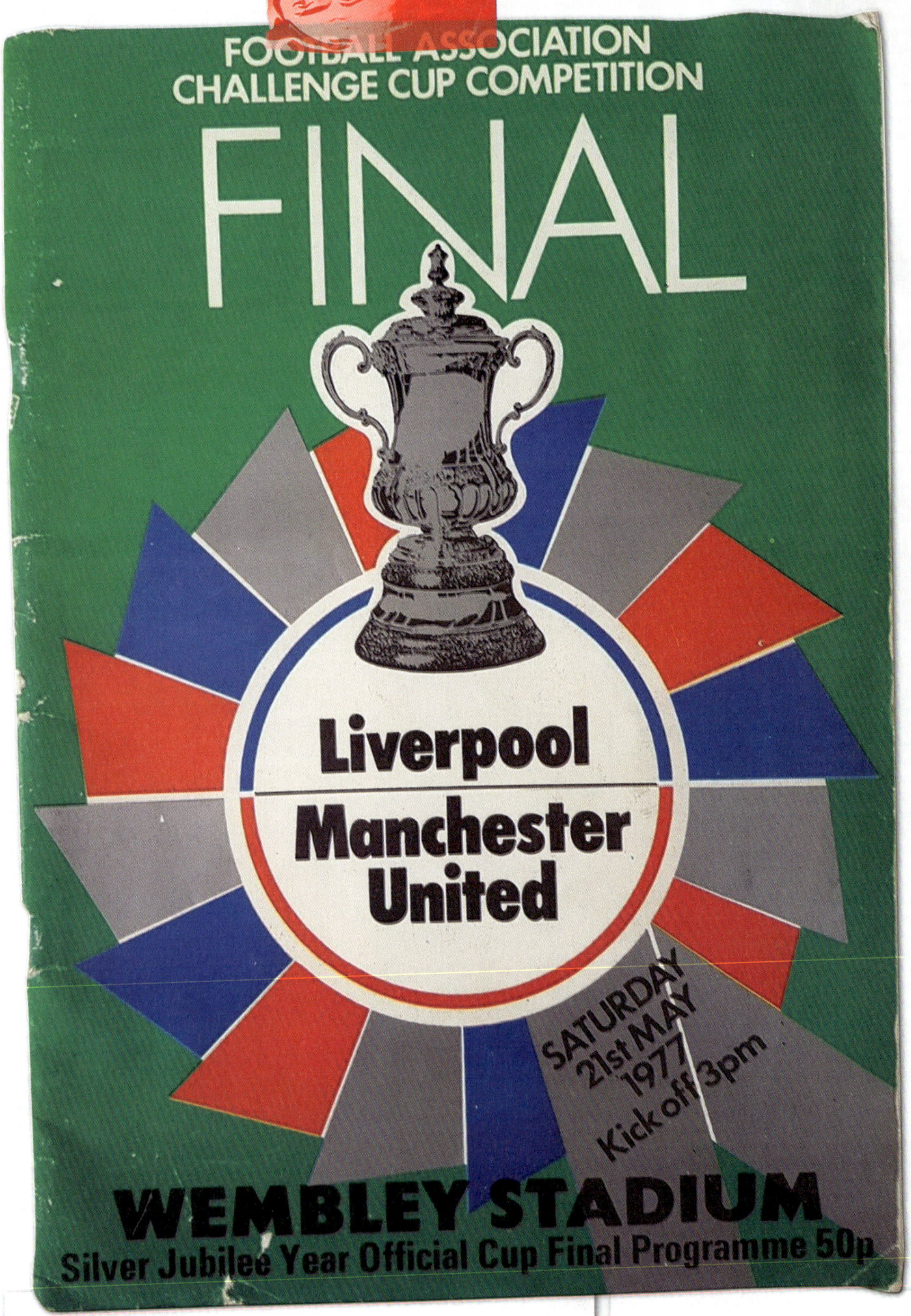

The drought continued as they headed into the 1980s. The previous decade had been a disappointment. United had struggled to regain the sparkle of the Busby era and failed. The coming decade was not starting hopefully. Sexton was not the man to make the sparks fly again and the 1979/80 season was only a brief flicker; the lads could achieve but not quite get to the top under his leadership.

The team put in a solid performance all season. True, the bravado of the Docherty line up was missing, but when the final whistle was blown that season, United had finished second in a strong challenge for the title with Liverpool.

As so, often there had been distractions. Two people died when a wall collapsed at a game at Middlesborough and United fans were involved. A TV "World in Action" programme accused Louis Edwards, club Chairman, of irregular payments to players and corruption. Edwards was dead of a heart attack four weeks after the programme aired and the inquiries petered out. His son Martin took over as chairman.

Hoping for a new start, Dave Sexton's men were anxious to build on the success of the last season.

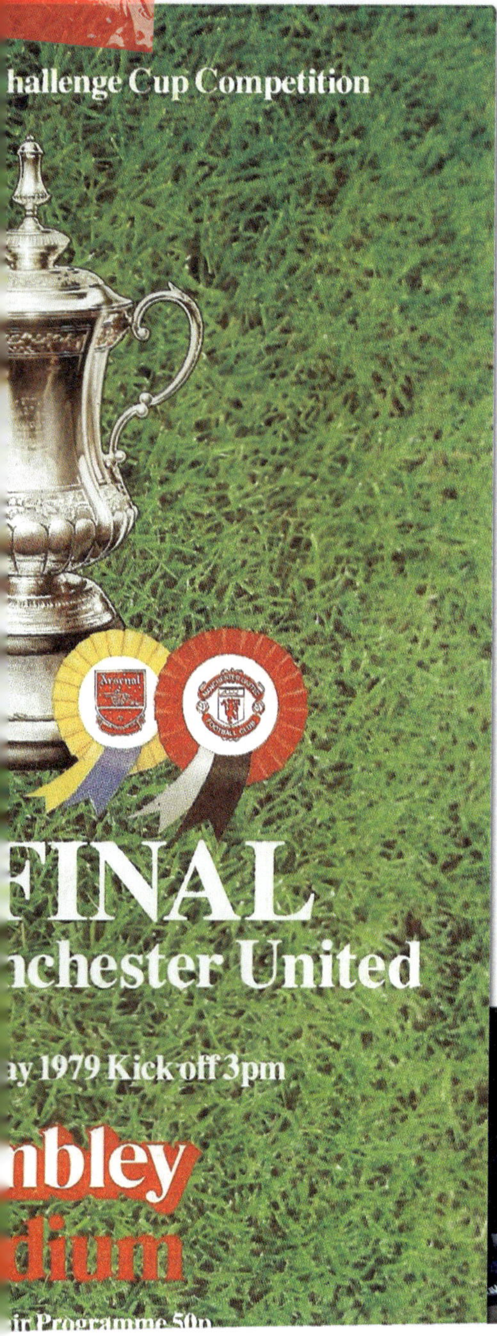

JOE JORDAN IN ACTION AGAINST FOREST 4TH OCTOBER 1980

MANCHESTER UNITED 1982/83 FA CUP, UNITED CELEBRATE FA CUP FINAL REPLAY VICTORY, 28TH MAY 1983

Kevin Moran and Mike Duxbury were new arrivals to watch but the steam ran out just after the season had started and Ray Wilkins was injured. The 18 draws typified the average nature of the season, 18 out of 42 games ended undecided. Sexton had signed Garry Birtles for 1.25 million but the player scored just one goal all season. The fans were staying away and the board decided to try for change again. When they chose they wanted strength. They got it in spades and showmanship to boot. Ron Atkinson had arrived.

The doors at the club swung to and fro as players

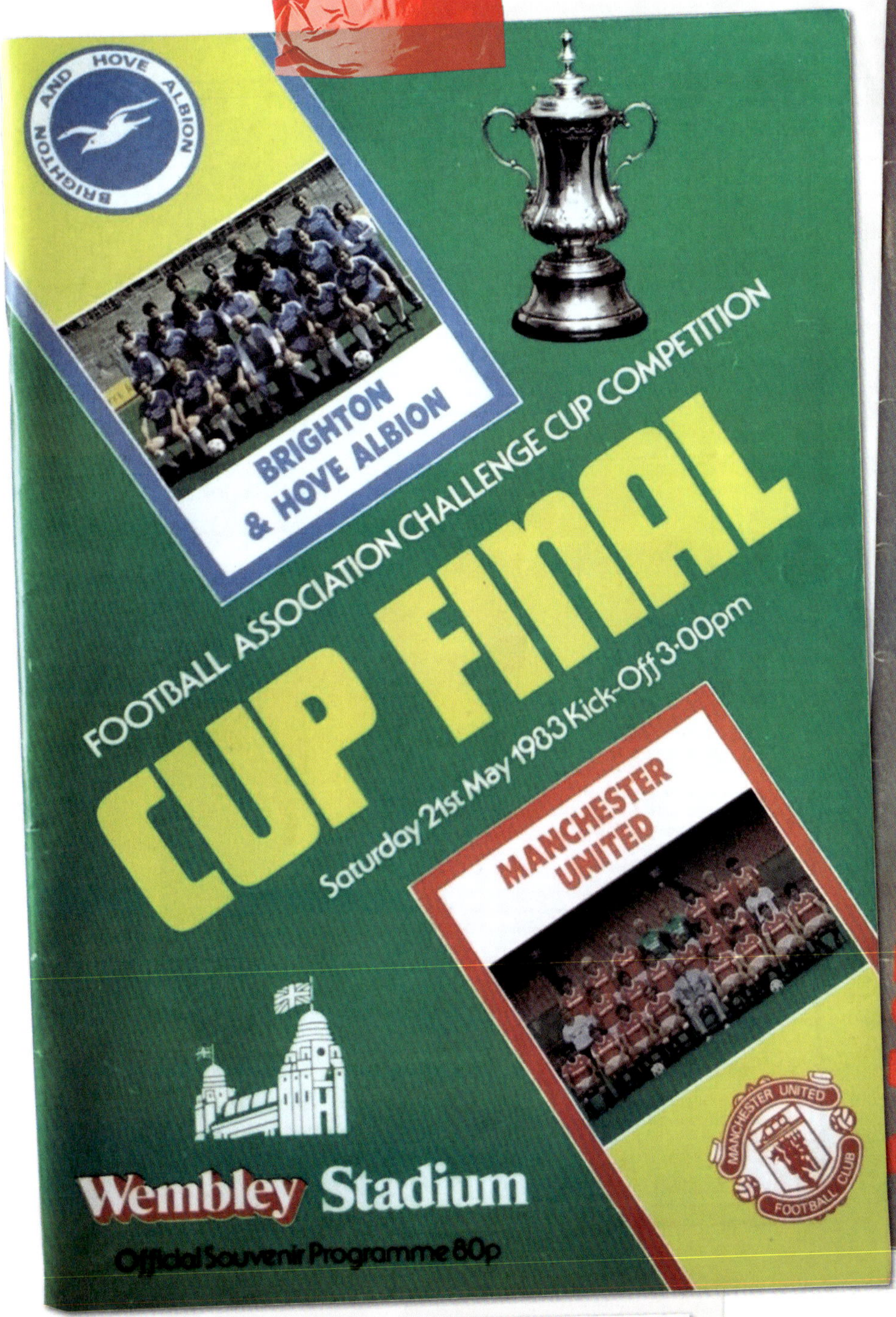

and back room boys came and went. Coaches Harry Gregg and Jack Crompton departed, Lou Macari and Sammy McIlroy were sidelined. Frank Stapleton came from Arsenal, Bryan Robson from West Brom and John Gidman from Everton. Robson, signed with Remi Moses for two million, soon became vital to the United team.

The new manager made his mark immediately and United found themselves at the top of the table in October thanks to two matches when they hit five goals each time. The League Cup was lost when Tottenham defeated them and the FA Cup dream faded when Second Division Watford pushed them out. Losing only 4 out of 24 matches showed that Atkinson's team was working well but they could not quite make the grade and at the end, Ipswich and Liverpool were above them in the league.

This was team that could take the club forward although there were not as many goals as the fans had once been used to: 59 in the league. Liverpool

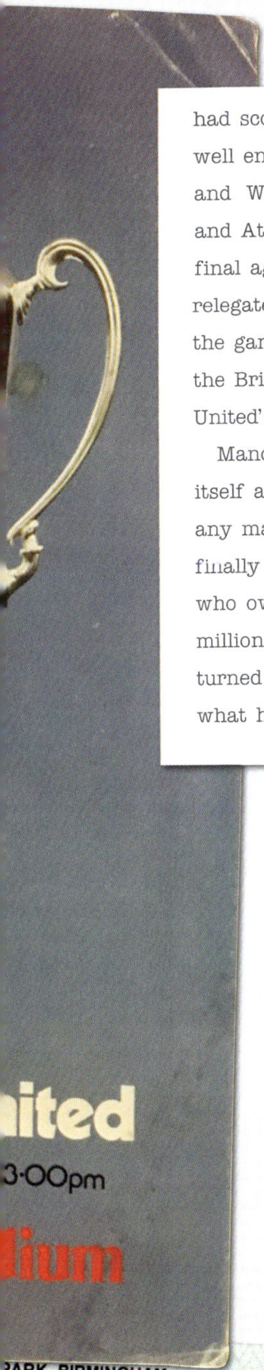

had scored 80. And a season that had begun well ended with a third place behind Liverpool again and Watford. Cup elation was waiting, however, and Atkinson steered his team into the FA Cup final against Brighton and Hove Albion who were relegated that season from Division One. United let the game slip with a 2-2 draw but soundly trounced the Brighton lads in the replay 4-0 and the cup was United's for the fifth time in their history.

Manchester's history however, wanted to repeat itself and Atkinson's follow up season failed to make any marks despite a positive beginning, with United finally slipping to fifth in the table. Robert Maxwell, who owned Oxford United, was said to be offering ten million to take over the Manchester club but the board turned the offer down. Now Atkinson had to wonder what he could pull out of the bag.

BRYAN ROBSON, 1984/85

In 1984/85 his trick was not to win the league; United only clambered back up to 4th position with both Everton and Liverpool above them. The warning signs had been seen as early as the second league defeat, a 5-0 drubbing at the hands of Everton. And there was nothing to lift the Reds' spirits until the FA Cup final. Atkinson may have found his chair wobbling if the Red Devils had not come through with the trophy beating Everton 1-0 this time.

The tragedies of the Bradford City Stadium fire and the Heysel Stadium disaster that year left gloom over the football world. United could only hope that next season would bring back their spark.

It did not. In fact, they laboured for their 4th place in the league and with performances such at the one against Third Division Bournemouth, a 2-0 defeat that had fans singing anti-Atkinson songs, they floundered in all the trophy challenges too.

Atkinson was to have one last bite at the cherry. With 10 wins to start the season, it looked as though the magic had returned and United shot ten points clear in the league. Goals might come from any number of players and the defence was tight. Atkinson was looking for new signings and then United hit the wall. The losses began and with two defeats in the final six games, they were six points below West Ham, who had pushed them out of the FA Cup, on fourth place at the season's end.

Atkinson could not find a way to revive the team's performance and when the first three games in the new 1986/87 season were lost, Atkinson's days were numbered. United slumped to 19th in the league. Atkinson was sacked the day after defeat in the League Cup to Southampton, 4-1.

In the middle of the despondency, no one would have believed that a major sea change had taken place when just one day after the sacking, another manager was on board. Alex Ferguson.

Ferguson's task was unenviable and he took the risk of relying on his tactics on the field and improving the attitude of available players to try to slow the fall. He watched whilst his men clawed their way back up to 11th by which time Ferguson had helped

WEMBLEY, (1-0) FA CUP FINAL, MANCHESTER UNITED CELEBRATE WITH CUP AFTER BEATING EVERTON, 18TH MAY 1985

ALEX FERGUSON MEETING MANCHESTER UNITED FANS, 22 NOVEMBER 1986

MANCHESTER UNITED V LIVERPOOL, NORMAN WHITESIDE DOES BATTLE, 28TH FEBUARY 1987

them to beat champions Liverpool. The same eight men played in the first games of the season and the last. The difference could only be the man in charge. The fans approved. But Ferguson was not to have an easy ride.

He did get the Reds back up the league to second place behind the dreaded Liverpool again next season so the team had obviously improved dramatically, and they had drawn 3-3 with the champions to prove it. And 31 goals from McClair, the best score since the unmatched George Best on 32 was a good sign. He had not produced any silverware and that did not sit well with United fans. Ferguson knew he had to improve or his time as manager would be short lived.

As has happened so often in United's history, the expectations rose only to be cruelly crushed almost immediately. The 1988/89 season proved to be one in a long line of those that were best forgotten. Ferguson began to exchange the players. 27 had a chance to prove themselves. And the results started to come in. Draw after draw and a team that could only get itself to 11th place in the league. There had been good moments but just three successes in twelve matches was not the stuff champions are made of. Many fans were again staying away.

With the 90s around the corner, Manchester seemed unable to move themselves consistently in the right

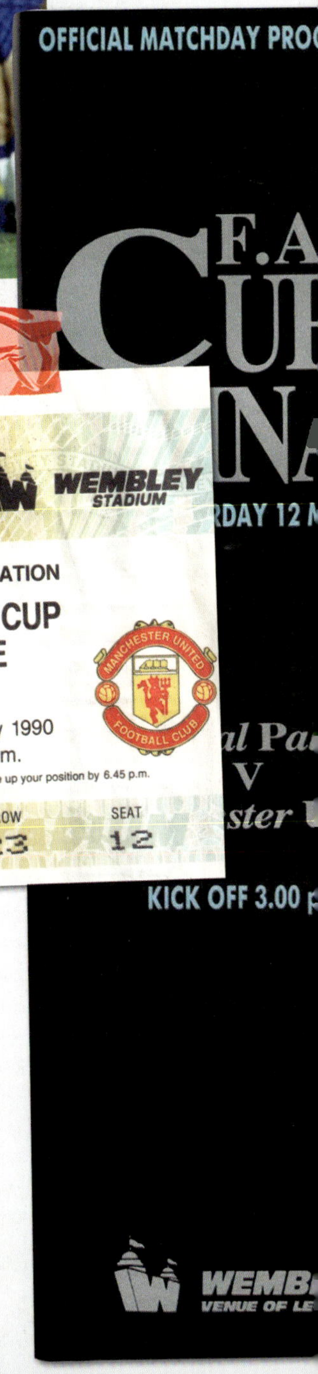

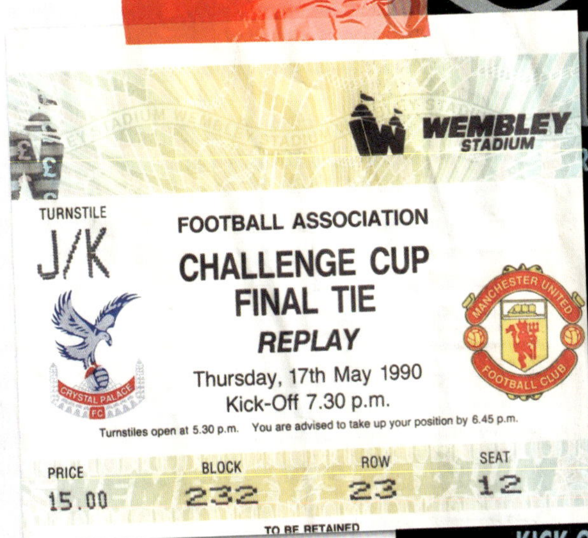

direction. Ferguson, it seemed, was the same as the other managers. He could produce one good season and then only mediocrity.

So the 1989/90 was going to be pivotal. And it was a cliff-hanger for Ferguson. On paper his results made him a candidate for the axe; United struggled in the league and managed a lamentable 13th place after their final game. Managers had departed for less. No one knows, or no one is telling, if one match saved Ferguson's career at United and enabled the club's glory-filled future. If it did, and Bobby Charlton denies that Ferguson's job was insecure, then that match was the FA Cup match against Nottingham Forest, in January 1990. It was agony for the fans and Ferguson. But the team crept through to the final; a 3-3 draw against Crystal Palace. And a 1-0 victory in the replay. Ferguson had his first trophy and he wasn't going anywhere for the foreseeable future.

The tide had turned, and United were heading for a future filled with extraordinary achievement. And the proof that United with Ferguson at the helm

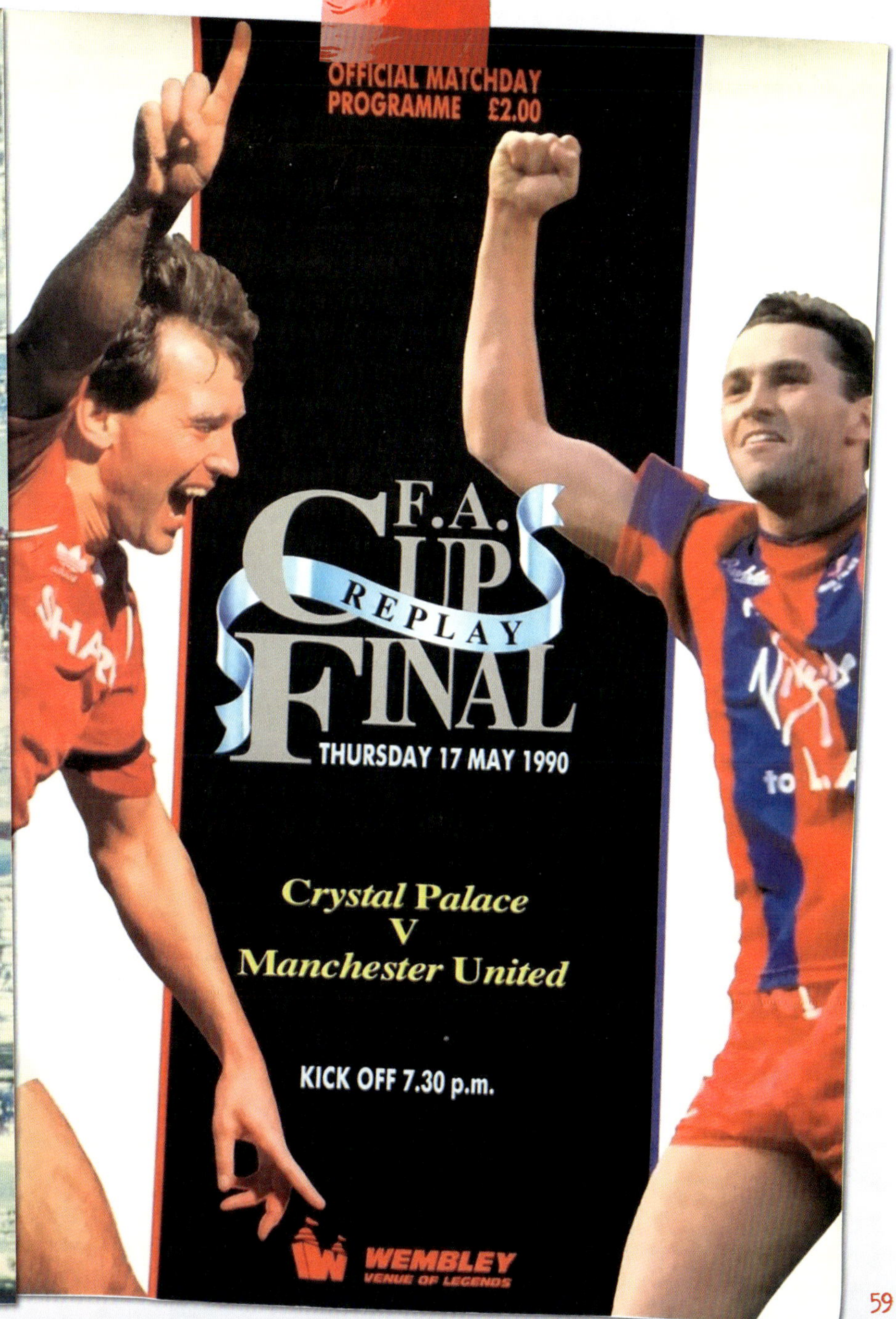

were onto something out of the ordinary came the very next season. This was the season when winger Ryan Giggs, a player creating as much excitement as George Best, signed his professional contract with the club. United still made heavy weather of the league, unable to get past Arsenal, Liverpool or Manchester City, and although they got to the League Cup Final, they lost 1-0 to Sheffield Wednesday. But there was still excitement for the fans to celebrate; in the UEFA Cup Winners Cup they fought their way through to the final, and in May 1991 came home victorious having beaten Barcelona 2-1.

Now the team went from strength to strength. They were to remain in the top three in the league until Alex Ferguson left in 2013. The manager made a major signing with Danish keeper Peter Schmeichel, the "bargain of the century" as Ferguson put it. And 22 clean sheets helped him to the title of, "The World's Best Goalkeeper 1992" proving Ferguson's point.

At the end of the 1991/92 season they were second in the league, having lost three consecutive games out of the last four, but had won the League Cup Final 1-0 against Nottingham Forest and also lifted the UEFA Super Cup. Ferguson was turning up the pressure and the fans were delighted.

Then, in the 1992/93 season, he helped the Old

Trafford boys realise the dream that had been put on hold for so long. There was no European silverware, and the FA and League cups went elsewhere; but United were top of the newly formed FA Premier League, 10 points ahead of Aston Villa on 74 points. They had finished the season with a ten-game, undefeated flourish with Mark Hughes as top goalscorer on 16, and Ryan Giggs proving his brilliance by bringing in his second PFA Young Player of the Year Award. And this season had seen the birth of another legend at Old Trafford: Eric Cantona had signed from Leeds United.

Ferguson had gathered a team to beat the world. And beat the world they would, but they began their domination of English football during the 1993/94 season by scooping the Charity Shield, then the FA Cup, when they wiped Chelsea off the pitch 4-0 with Cantona hammering home two penalties, and by taking the Premiership once again with 92 points, 8 points clear of Blackburn Rovers.

And then, as though the gods wanted to teach them a lesson, they missed everything they aimed for the following season except the Charity Shield as a weak

↑ MANCHESTER UNITED MANAGER ALEX FERGUSON HOLDS THE PREMIERSHIP TROPHY WITH HIS ASSISTANT BRIAN KIDD, 3RD MAY 1993

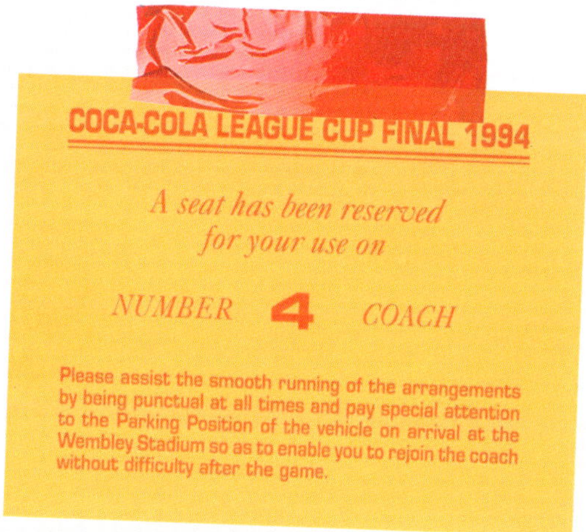
COCA-COLA LEAGUE CUP FINAL 1994

A seat has been reserved for your use on

NUMBER **4** COACH

Please assist the smooth running of the arrangements by being punctual at all times and pay special attention to the Parking Position of the vehicle on arrival at the Wembley Stadium so as to enable you to rejoin the coach without difficulty after the game.

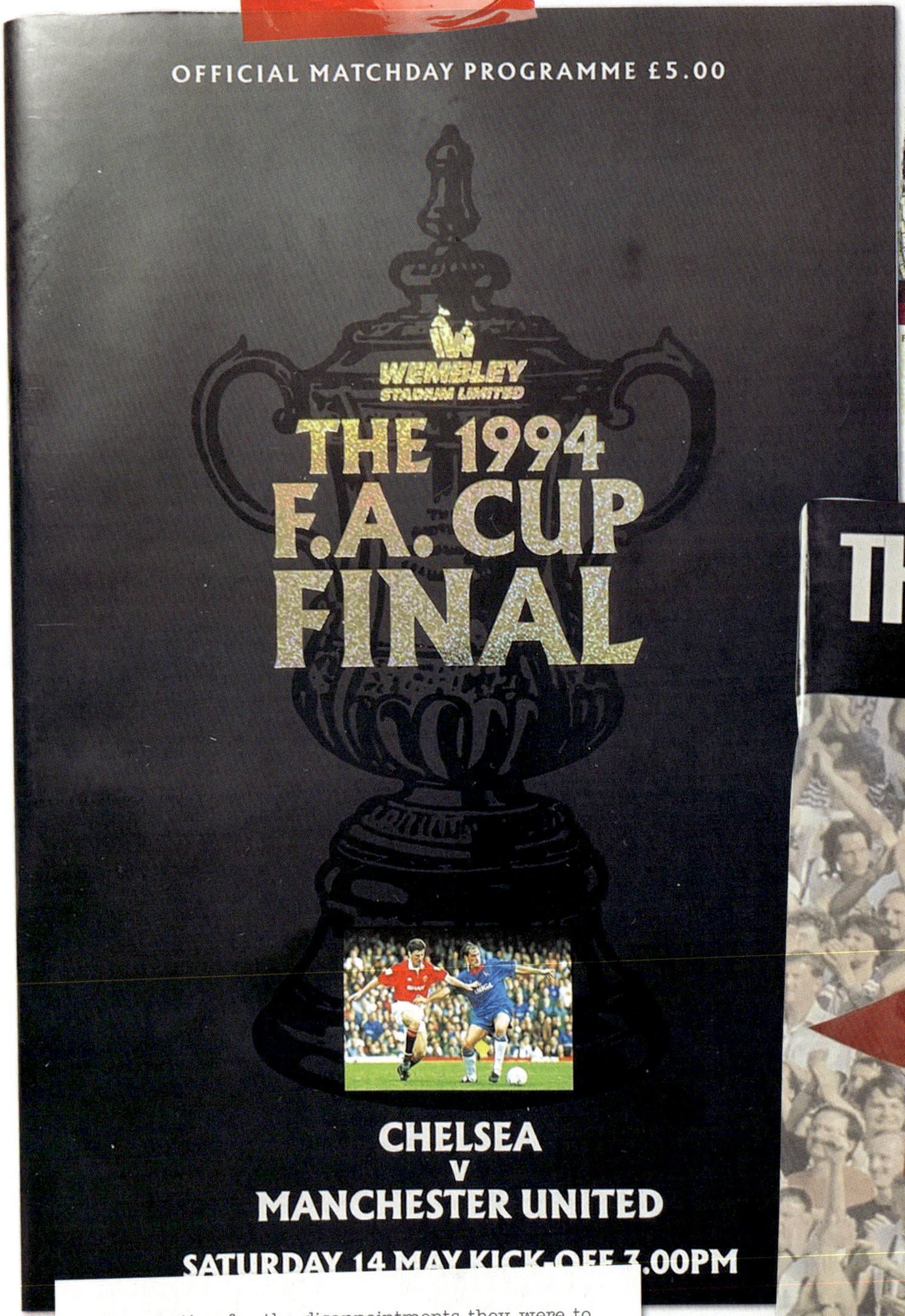

compensation for the disappointments they were to experience. The coveted third consecutive league title was snatched from them by Blackburn Rovers by one point; 88 to 89 and the FA Cup Final was lost to Everton 1-0. The fun of the 9-0 walloping of lowly Ipswich Town in March had been long forgotten.

So when Alex Ferguson started out in the 1995/96 season, he still had a lot to prove. Another lethal weapon had by now been added to the Manchester armoury and this one meant business. He joined the 1990's group of youngsters known as "Fergie's

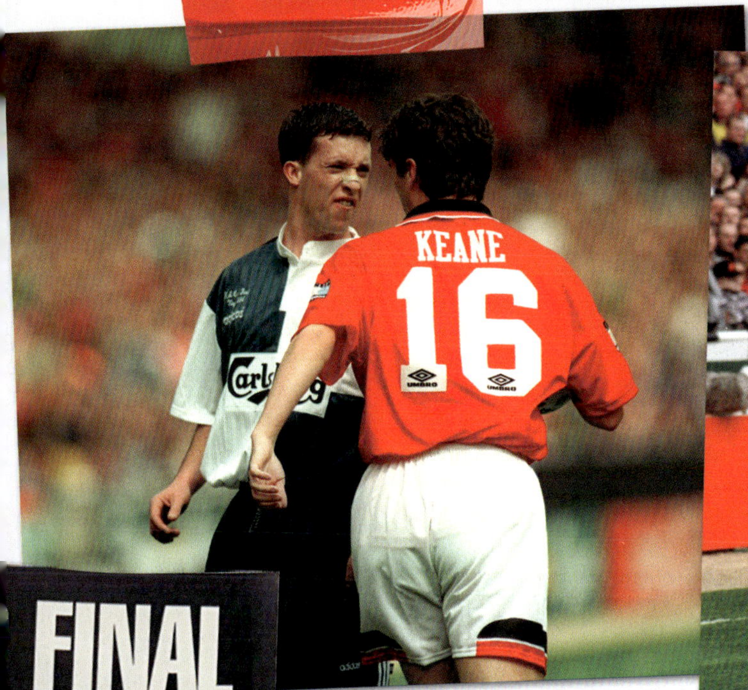

1996 FA CUP FINAL, AGAINST LIVERPOOL, ROY KEANE TAKES ON ROBBIE FOWLER & STEVE MCMANAMAN, 11TH MAY 1996

Fledglings", players such as Nicky Butt, Ryan Giggs, Paul Scholes, Phil Neville and Gary Neville. The new boy's name was David Beckham.

Once Fergie's lads had pulled off that double in the 1995/96 season - memorable, too, of course, for that spectacular Beckham goal against Wimbledon when he struck the ball from the halfway line - winning both the Premiership and the FA Cup Final, there would never be a need for proof of Fergie's abilities ever again.

True to his philosophy of long-term thinking, Ferguson was still building his side so the next two seasons were slightly less fulfilling. United won the league for the second consecutive season in 1996/97 having pulled in the Charity Shield, too, a trick they repeated the following season (making it four Shields in five seasons) one unsettlingly devoid of any top places. They were second in the league just one point behind Arsenal who had 78.

AH, BUT FOR WHAT CAME NEXT IT WAS WORTH WADING THROUGH AN OUT-OF-SORTS SEASON.

It's Autumn 1998 and United start out on a historic

F.A. CUP FINAL 1996
SPONSORED BY LITTLEWOODS
WEMBLEY
STADIUM LIMITED
F.A. CUP
LITTLEWOODS
LIVERPOOL
V
MANCHESTER
UNITED
SATURDAY 11 MAY 1996
KICK OFF 3.00p.m.
OFFICIAL MATCHDAY PROGRAMME £6.00

FUTEBOL CLUBE DO PORTO
MANCHESTER UNITED
CHAMPIONS LEAGUE
Porta
Sector
Fila
TER UNITED SUPPORTERS

UEFA Champions League
Mercredi 4 mars
20 h 45
A.S. MONACO
MANCHESTER UNITED F.C.
STADE LOUIS II - MONACO
Division
Catégorie
Rang
Place
DIVISION
CATEGORIE
RANG
PLACE
SECONDES
F2
2
57
PT 150.00 F
000830

MANCHESTER UNITED
036 AS MONACO
UEFA CHAMPIONS LEAGUE QF2
WED 18/03/98
KICK OFF: 7.45PM
ADULT
£19.00
T/NO: 03100127
MR HOWARD M DAVIES
North Stand Tier 1 Upper
ENTRANCE N43
BLOCK N2405
ROW 27
SEAT 0187
UEFA
CHAMPIONS LEAGUE

1996 FA CUP FINAL, ALEX FERGUSON CONGRATULATES ERIC CANTONA 11TH MAY 1996

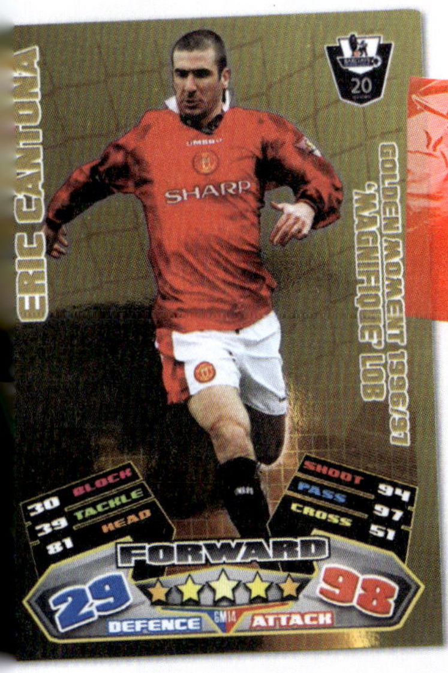

season, the most successful season in their history. Dutch defender Jaap Stam had joined their ranks as had Dwight Yorke, who was to embark on an unforgettable season for United, in which, with 29 goals, he became top goalscorer: as, indeed, he did the following season.

It had all started badly with a 3-0 defeat to Arsenal in the Charity Shield and the league games started like a damp squib with two draws. When they lost to Arsenal again they dropped to 10th place. There were only to be three more losses, however and from December of 1998 United completed a 20 game undefeated run to the end of the season despite some close run games, notably against Arsenal and Liverpool but including a 6-2 cheering-festival against Leicester. Their never-say-die attitude brought them the Premiership title, a reverse of the previous year with Manchester on 79 points, one ahead of Arsenal. They added the FA Cup with a 2-0 win against Newcastle United, and then came their pièce de résistance.

The 26th of May 1999. The opponent, the feared Germans from Bayern Munich. It's the UEFA Champions League Final, which United have arrived at via Barcelona, Inter Milan and Juventus, just to show the standard of football they were playing.

United went one goal down and stayed there to half time, always in danger of conceding a second. As the match progressed there were brilliant chances on both sides, heart-stopping moments until ten minutes before time, striker Ole Gunnar Solskjær was brought on. In extra time, a messy Bayern penalty area saw Sheringham hit the equaliser.

BUT THE EXCITEMENT GOT WORSE.

77
J267A0
GOL NORD 2 GRADERIA
CHAMPIONS LEAGUE
MANCHESTER UNITED FC
v
FC BAYERN MUNCHEN
MANCHESTER UNITED FC
021147
PRECIO/PREU: 7000
FILA/FILA: 0029 ASIENTO/SEIENT: 0001
BOCA/BOCA:345
PUERTA/PORTA:

BAD IMNAU
KULMBACH

UNITED TEAM LINE UP WITH THE EUROPEAN CUP TROPHY AFTER THEIR DRAMATIC WIN, 26TH MAY 1999

A United corner less than 45 seconds before the whistle found the foot of Solskjær and United were in the lead. The Bayern players were in shock. But it was true. United were the new champions of Europe.

AND FERGUSON WAS KNIGHTED FOR HIS SERVICES TO FOOTBALL.

The Premiership was theirs again in the new millennium as they won their final eleven games to romp home ahead of Arsenal, 91 points to 73. Back in Europe, they were runners up in the Super Cup losing to Lazio 0-1 but found more success in the Intercontinental Cup where they played Brazilian team Palmeiras and emerged victorious with a Roy Keane goal.

They completed a three-in-a-row stack of Premiership titles in 2001, once again they beat Arsenal to the top place with 80 points to 70 having beaten them by a whopping 6-1 in February, and despite an extraordinary three back-to-back losses to finish the season, which just proved their domination.

There were, however, no other honours that year for fans to enthuse about in the pubs and schoolyards of Manchester and the next season efforts produced even less; nothing better than a runners-up tag in the Charity Shield; 2-1 to Liverpool.

Still, a new hero had arrived to thrill the fans; Dutch striker Rutgerus Johannes Martinus "Ruud" van Nistelrooy was now wearing red, and his success - top goalscorer in four of the next five seasons - soon brought Sheringham's career in red to an end. Van Nistelrooy scored an astonishing 44 goals in the 2002/03 season, a United record that has not been surpassed to this day.

There was to be only one Premiership title in the next five seasons; in 2003, the year in which Cristiano Ronaldo made his debut. Ferguson was gradually putting together a team of superlatives and had now netted a man often referred to as the best player in the world.

In 2004, the man who was to break Bobby Charlton's goal-scoring record - on the 21st of January 2017, he scored his 250th goal - arrived at Old Trafford aged just 18 and announced his talent with a hat-trick on his debut. He was Wayne Rooney. Old Trafford had a new football God.

The FINAL
MANCHESTER UNITED v MILLWALL
OFFICIAL MATCHDAY PROGRAMME £8.50
3PM SATURDAY, 22 MAY 2004
MILLENNIUM STADIUM, CARDIFF
CUP TheFA CUP
CUP TheFA CUP
NSPCC
Cruelty to children must stop. FULL STOP.
50 pence of the cover value of each match programme sold at The FA Cup Final on 22 May 2004 will be donated to the NSPCC
Registered charity number 216401

CRISTIANO RONALDO
7
WEIGHT 75KG HEIGHT 184CM
APPEARANCES FOR MAN UTD
98
GOALS FOR MAN UTD
16
INTERNATIONAL CAPS
23
INTERNATIONAL GOALS
9
TIME AT CLUB (YEARS/MONTHS)
2/0
YEAR OF BIRTH
1985
This Portuguese International joined United from Sporting Lisbon in a £12.24 million deal in August 2003. Ronaldo entered professional football at the age of 17 and has not looked back, he continues to progress and adapt to the English game improving his skills with every match.
POSITION FORWARD
PREVIOUS CLUB SPORTING LISBON

RUUD VAN NISTELROOY
HEIGHT (CM)
188
WEIGHT (KG)
79
GOALS AT UNITED
84
APPEARANCES
110
YEAR OF BIRTH
1976
CAPS
27
vodafone
SIGNED FROM PSV EINDHOVEN, HOLLAND
NATION: HOLLAND
POSITION OF PLAY: FORWARD
SQUAD NUMBER: 10

CRISTIANO RONALDO TRIES A SHOT DURING THE FA CUP MATCH AGAINST MANCHESTER CITY AT OLD TRAFFORD, 14TH FEBRUARY 2004

Ironically, with the advent of Rooney, Europe receded for a few years, but the season gave fans something to shout about, nonetheless, when the FA Cup fell into Manchester's hands - 3-0 against humble Millwall - after the, renamed Community Shield had been denied to Arsenal in a penalty shoot out. The Premiership performance had been poor, and the best they could manage in the second half of it was two unbeaten games in a row.

Patience was needed, then, and another year of drought was mercifully killed off in 2005/06 with a 4-0 League Cup victory against Wigan Athletic.

Roy Keane had called it a day long before then; he ended his career at Old Trafford in September 2005 where he had been since 1993. And one week later, the incomparable George Best passed away aged 59.

When the Premiership turned red again in 2007, it was a welcome but sole reward for the lads' efforts. That, however, was about to change dramatically and United entered upon one of the most successful periods in their history. For Ferguson it would usher in the final phase of his management and shower the Reds in glory. By 2013, all the major silverware he won had been augmented by five Community Shield victories in seven outings.

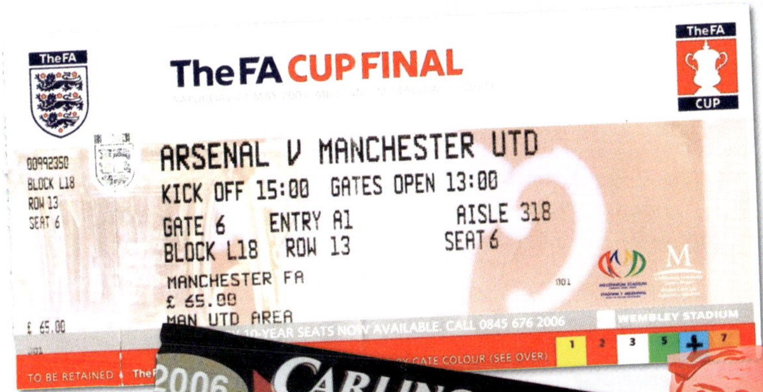

ROONEY CELEBRATES AFTER SCORING AGAINST EVERTON, DURING THEIR PREMIERSHIP MATCH AT GOODISON PARK, 28TH APRIL 2007

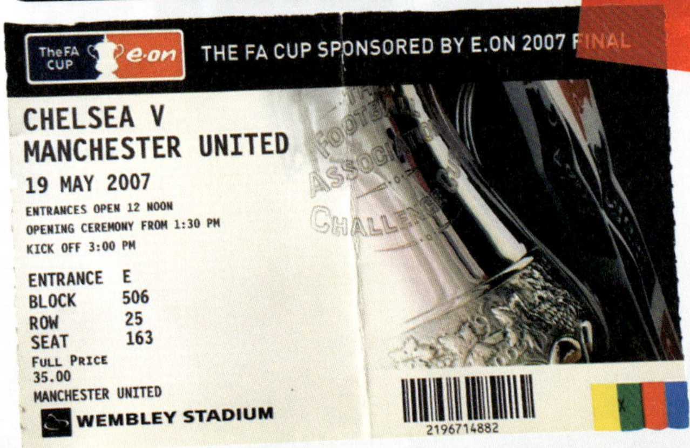

Two more Premiership titles successively came United's way as they left first Chelsea and then Liverpool behind, before conquering Europe again, brushing aside Barcelona and winning the UEFA Champions League Final in 2008 against Chelsea, in a 6-5 penalty shoot-out after a 1-1 draw. A fitting close to a season that marked the 50th anniversary of the Munich air disaster.

Ronaldo scored a personal best at United with 42 goals that season.

YET THERE WAS EVEN BETTER TO COME FOR THE TEAM.

In 2008/09, United took the Treble of the Premiership, with 90 points, four points clear of Liverpool, the Football League Cup, 4-1 on penalties against Tottenham, and the FIFA Club World Cup, the first English club to do so; 1-0 against LDU Quito. There was enough, then, to make up for the semi-final losses in both the Champions League (against old foes Barcelona) and in the UEFA Super Cup. United had become the first club to win the Premiership three times in a row on two separate occasions and the inimitable Ronaldo celebrated his third consecutive season as top goalscorer, with 26 goals.

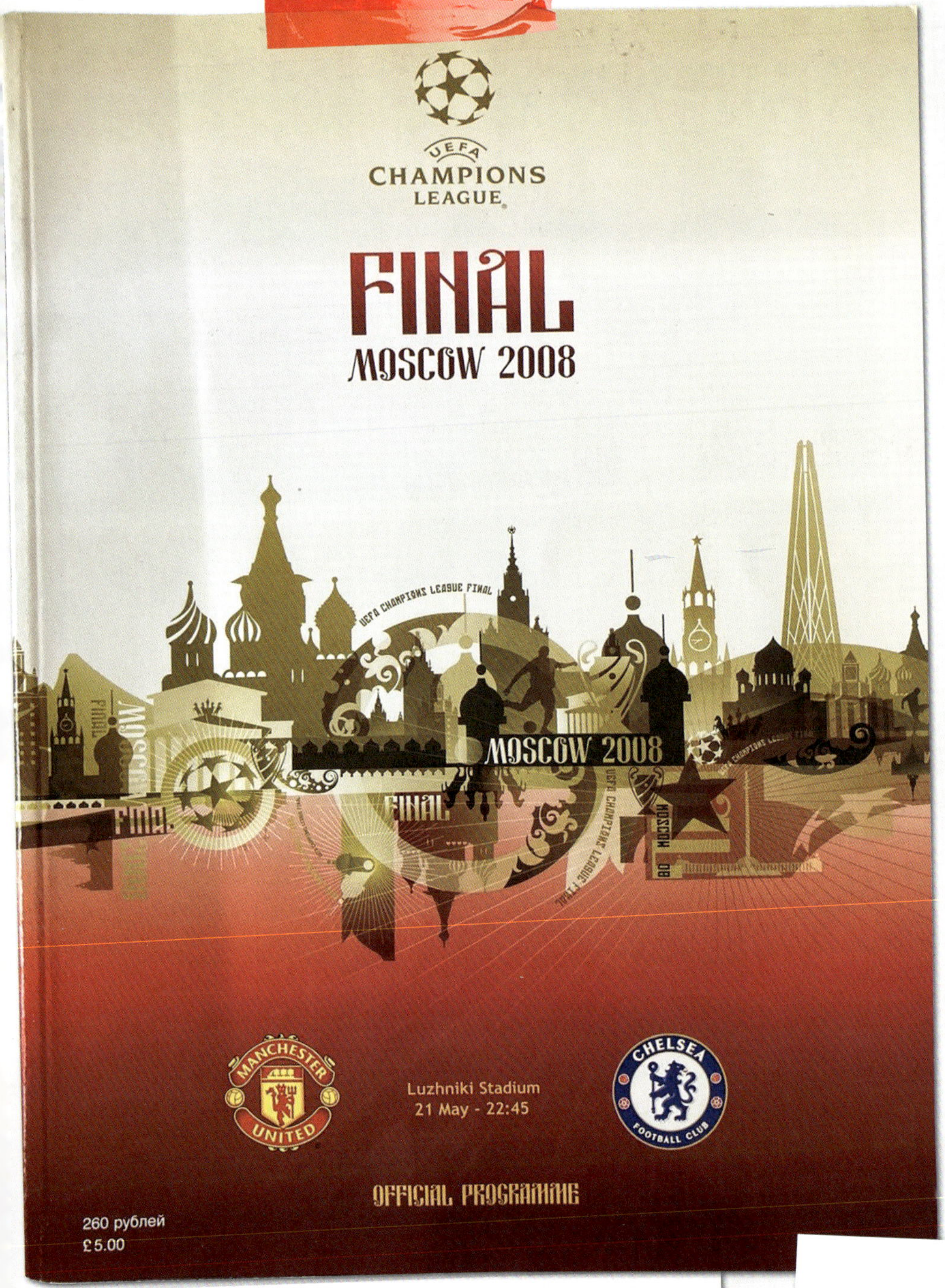

SO THE TANTALISING THOUGHT WAS WHAT TREATS MIGHT LIE IN STORE FOR THE FOLLOWING SEASON.

NOT TOO MUCH, IN FACT.

As happens so often in football, expectations were high and not fulfilled as hoped. Wayne Rooney had a good season, his 34 goals giving him top goalscorer spot for the third time. United were winners of the League Cup putting two past Aston Villa's one, to give them their fourth League Cup title. Everything else escaped them. Only just, but that's all it takes between champion and runner-up. Too many league losses meant that Chelsea, who had beaten United twice 1-2 and 0-1, pipped them at the post by one point; 86

BLEY STADIUM
day 01 March 2009
CK OFF 3PM ENTRANCE OPENS 1PM
TRANCE E
LOCK ROW SEAT
02 28 34
£52.00
Man Utd
ORDER # 482598
THE FOOTBALL LEAGUE
ING CUP
FINAL2009
CAR
MANCHESTER UNITED
TOTTENHAM HOTSPUR

£9 €10
UEFA CHAMPIONS LEAGUE
OFFICIAL PROGRAMME
ROMA
FINALE 2009
27 May 20:45 Stadio Olimpico

Audi Cup
29.07.2009
FC Bayern München
AC Mailand
CA Boca Juniors
Manchester United FC
Allianz Arena München
Halbfinale 1 und Halbfinale 2
Südtribüne Oberrang Kat. 4
€ 25,00
Vollzahler
310 14 17

CHAMPIONS BISTRO
WEDNESDAY
LUNCH
27 MAY 2009, 12:00 – 16:00
P
ROMA FINALE 2009

CHAMPIONS LEAGUE
ROMA FINALE 2009
FOR SEATING PURPOSE ONLY
TRIBUNA STAMPA INFERIORE
39 3
SECTOR
COMMENTARY POSITION
SEAT

to 85. The Blues also denied them the Community Shield, winning 4-1 on penalties. And that was it, somewhat of a comedown after the previous year.

And, in fact, there was no more joy to be had in Europe in subsequent years, either. And there would be five seasons when the FA Cup and League cups would go elsewhere which could not be felt as anything other than a let down after a string of thrilling successes dating back to 1990.

Fortunately, United's form in the Premiership came to their rescue in the 2010/11 season and Chelsea were pushed back into second place on 71 points, way behind United's 80 points. They were well-deserved winners after a 24-game undefeated run from the beginning of the season: a season in which, amongst the heavy hitters, they only suffered losses to Chelsea, 1-2, Arsenal, 0-1, and Liverpool, 1-3.

In 2012, United once again came away empty-handed from all the big competitions and it was especially galling to lose the Premiership to arch rivals Manchester City, who snatched the title in the last game of the season with two late goals, leaving both clubs on 89 points but City winning with a superior goal difference. It left all the extraordinary victories - four 5-0 wins against Bolton Wanderers, Fulham, Wigan Athletic and Wolverhampton Wanderers and the extraordinary 8-2 humiliation of Arsenal, which saw Rooney put away a hat trick, as hollow victories.

Alex Ferguson was already reading the writing on the wall by this time as he looked back over the past three seasons. He had decided that 2012/13 was the end of the road for him. Thankfully, and fittingly for such a giant of the English and Scottish football leagues, his reign at Old Trafford ended with a final victory and an eighteen-match undefeated run. And Ferguson's managerial career ended on a quirky note; in the final game of the season against West Bromwich Albion the two teams went home after a 5-5 draw; it was a record, the first time two Premier League teams had scored five goals each. United bade farewell to their unrivalled manager with 89 points to Manchester City's 78.

AND THAT WAS IT. THE DAY THAT NO ONE COULD IMAGINE CAME AND WENT AS FERGUSON LEFT THE MANAGER'S BENCH FOR THE LAST TIME. AN INCREDIBLE TWENTY-SEVEN YEAR RED BLAZE HAD COME TO AN END.

SIR ALEX FERGUSON GESTURES TO THE UNITED FANS, AFTER THE WEST BROM PREMIER LEAGUE MATCH AT THE HAWTHORNS STADIUM, 19TH MAY 2013

A PERIOD OF ADJUSTMENT

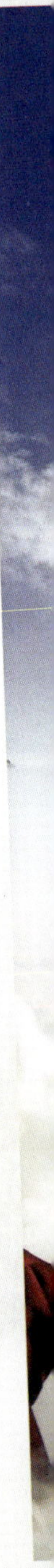

On the 1st of July, David Moyes took over the great man's place; his six-year contract looked rather silly just ten months later when, after poor results, he was fired and Ryan Giggs was appointed as interim player-manager to pick up the pieces. At the end of that season, all that United had won was the FA Community Shield, 2-0 against Wigan Athletic. Worse, United had finished the Premiership season in seventh place, their worst placing since 1990. This was also the first time United hadn't qualified for a European competition since 1990. Moyes' place was then taken by Louis van Gaal and Giggs was retained as his assistant. It was truly the end of an era when Malcolm Glazer died on the 28th of May 2014.

It was as though everything had gone on hold at Old Trafford. Van Gaal was able to staunch the flow of blood during his first season in charge, in the Premiership, at least, with United finishing in fourth place but 17 points adrift of the leaders, Chelsea. So, when Van Gaal was unable to salvage the Premiership in 2015/16 - they came 5th - the third failure in three years, and despite winning the FA Cup for the twelfth time with a 1-2 defeat of Crystal Palace, the managers' door revolved again - and in walked none other than José Mourinho. The former Chelsea whizz kid had long eyed Manchester as a club that he would like to manage. What could he pull out of the bag against a resurgent Chelsea and Liverpool, Arsenal and Manchester City?

After a hopeful start, winning the Community Shield 2-1 against Leicester and three Premiership victories, United began to struggle. But then, they had struggled when Ferguson took over, and building a quality team requires patience, understanding, time and managerial strength. They went through a sticky period when they won just two games out of eleven and slid to 8th in the league. At that point, Mourinho was able to pull the rudder around and, finally, some of the old sparks returned.

In fact, there were a record-breaking 25 games without defeat to take them through to the 30th of April 2017. But that run hid the problems. 12 of the games had ended in draws. The team had not been able to break the stranglehold of either Chelsea or Tottenham and had been unable to get higher than fifth during the long unbeaten run. As a result, they lost contact with the top four and the season ended with the Reds in 6th place.

There was no luck in the FA Cup run, either, as it ended at Chelsea in round 6 with a 1-0 defeat.

AND YET; IT'S ALWAYS A MISTAKE TO UNDERESTIMATE THE OLD TRAFFORD SIDE. THE SILVER LINING WAS WAITING.

There had been good news. In February, the team lifted the League Cup, now rebranded the EFL Cup, beating Southampton 3-2. It was a close run thing, though, with Southampton pushing into United constantly, and Ibrahimovic had to wait until the 87th minute to put the United fans

CHAMPIONS LEAGUE
ünchen
nited FC
4 20:45 Uhr
München
BLOCK REIHE PLATZ
304 14 12
UEFA.com

TO BE GIVEN UP
Standard Chartered
WARRIOR
www.liverpoolfc.com
BARCLAYS PREMIER LEAGUE
LIVERPOOL V MANCHESTER UNITED
Sunday 1st September 2013
KICKOFF 1.30PM
ANFIELD ROAD LOWER
Block Row Seat ADULT
124 32 0101 £48.00
TURNSTILE:N 1-2
Visitors Seating
LIVERPOOL FOOTBALL CLUB

CHAMPIONS LEAGUE
Manchester United FC vs Real Sociedad de Futbol
Old Trafford
Wed 23 Oct 2013, KO 7:45pm
East Stand Tier 1 Upper
Entrance Block Row Seat Price
E30 E230 25 88 £0.00
Master J Monteith
Comp (ST Cup Game)
UEFA.com

CHAMPIONS LEAGUE
"G. Karaiskakis" Stadium
Tue, 25/02/2014 21:45
OLYMPIACOS FC-MANCHESTER UNITED FC
UEFA Champions League 2013/14-Round of 16
ΘΥΡΑ GATE 11
ΣΕΙΡΑ ROW 07
ΘΕΣΗ SEAT 11
ΤΙΜΗ PRICE 90,00
10/02/2014 19:30
User: OSFPFCBO-3250275
Order: 6288753
Tic No: 24264634
KANONIKO
Account: 3370564
KANONIKO
UEFA.com
24264634-0

CHAMPIONS LEAGUE
UEFA Champions League
Bayer 04 Leverkusen - Manchester United FC
Datum: 27.11.13
BayArena, Bismarckstr. 122-124, 51373 Leverkusen
Anstoß: 20:45:00
Stadionöffnung: 19:15:00
Tribüne: NORD
Block: E2
Reihe: 26
Platz: 17
NORM
37,60
zzgl. Gebühren
UEFA.com

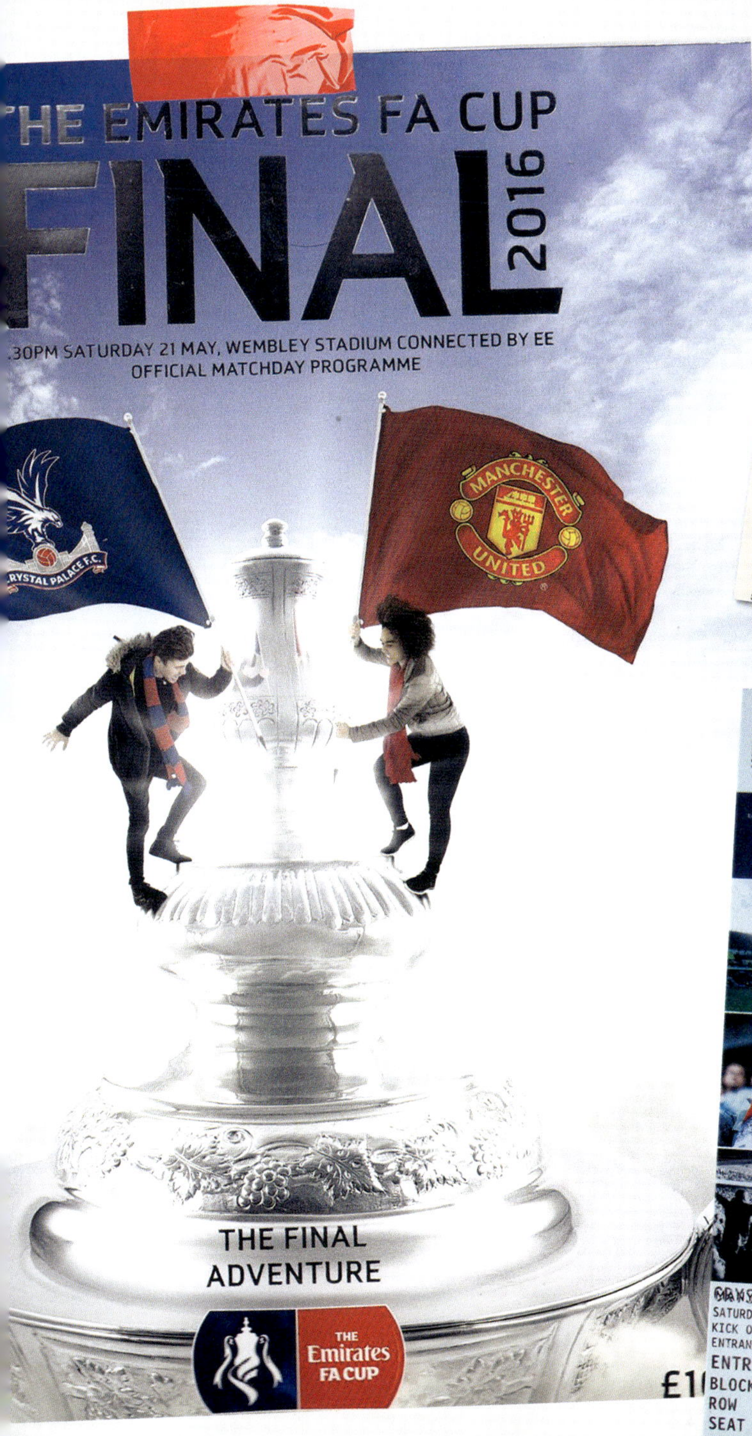
THE EMIRATES FA CUP
FINAL 2016
.30PM SATURDAY 21 MAY, WEMBLEY STADIUM CONNECTED BY EE
OFFICIAL MATCHDAY PROGRAMME
CRYSTAL PALACE F.C.
MANCHESTER UNITED
THE FINAL ADVENTURE
THE Emirates FA CUP

#EmiratesFACup
THE Emirates FA CUP
WEMBLEY
THE EMIRATES FA CUP FINAL 2016
SATURDAY 21 MAY 2016
KICK OFF 17:30
ENTRANCE OPENS 15:30
ENTRANCE G
BLOCK 105
ROW 5
SEAT 91
£ 85.00
TEAM EAST FULL PRICE
MANCHESTER UNITED SUPPORTERS ONLY
WEMBLEY CONNECTED BY EE

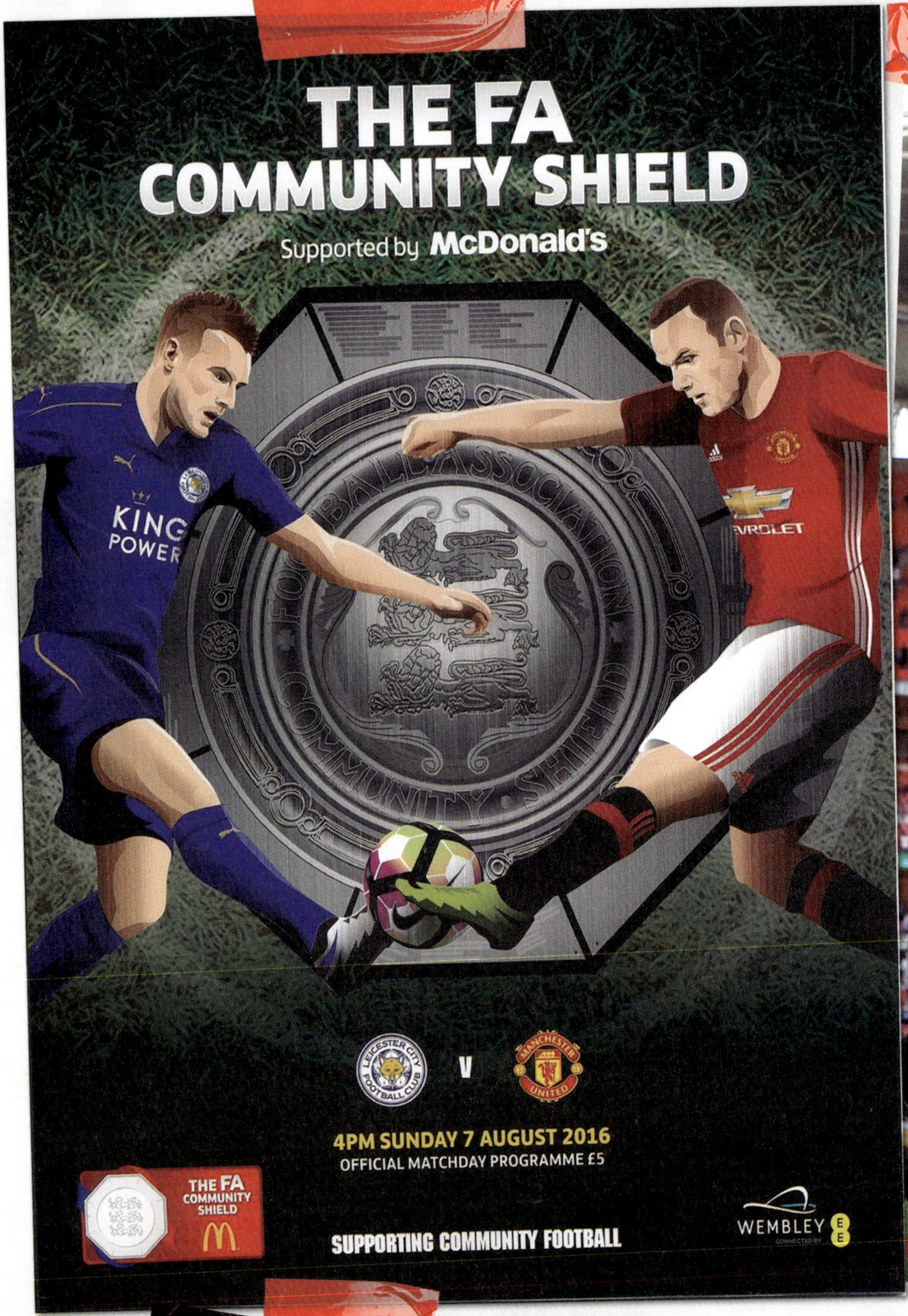

THE TEAM POSE WITH THE TROPHY AFTER THE FA COMMUNITY SHIELD MATCH AGAINST LEICESTER AT WEMBLEY STADIUM ON AUGUST 7, 2016

out of their agony and score the winning goal. The victory mado Manchester United the most successful English club, putting them above their northern rival Liverpool.

Zlatan Ibrahimovic would gain a personal reward for his persistence, because he finished his season as top goalscorer with 28 goals.

The league season had finished, but the excitement had not, for on the 24th May United walked out in the UEFA Europa League final against the Dutch club Ajax, also one of the most successful clubs in the world; a clash of giants. United had squeezed out Celta Vigo in the heart-stopping semi-final, managing to limit the damage to 2-1 and give the side confidence for the final.

Emotions were raw on the night of the final, but not for reasons that are normally associated with football matches. Just four days before, there had been a terrorist attack at a concert venue in Manchester that took the lives of 22 people. No one would have been surprised if the Reds had not won; not one of the fans would have been anything but

proud of their team that night anyway.

But the men from United showed that they are the stuff of champions and played as they always do; they played to win. Mourinho had told them to do it for the city, do it for the kids - and they did; the lads from the town played for the victims, played for the town and the club they were so proud of belonging to.

Although the young Ajax side set about the Reds with verve and had possession of the ball for a good of deal of the game, the experience of the Manchester lads shone through as they held fast together, and after just 18 minutes, Paul Pogba had the ball in the net after his low left-foot shot from just outside the penalty area was deflected over the Ajax keeper.

The second half had barely started when Henrikh Mkhitaryan flicked his right foot three yards out and the second goal was in. 2-0. United continued to defend superbly, kept the Dutch at bay, and that was the score for the remainder of the game.

There was a last-minute substitution in the shape of

Wayne Rooney, who came running on so that he would also be there to lift the trophy.

When the final whistle was blown, Manchester had ended their season as the 2017 UEFA Europa League Champions. A place in the UEFA Champions League competition for the next season was also theirs as was a match against the winners of the 2016-17 UEFA Champions League in the 2017 UEFA Super Cup.

Tears flowed, the stoic Mourinho was beaming and was bear-hugged by his son and... kissed the trophy! Yes, indeed, emotion and happiness were running high. The joy of success was more poignant because it was also intended for the people back home in Manchester, who had been given a sign that the Mancunian spirit was unbroken and unbowed.

Man of the match Ander Herrera said, “We want to dedicate it to all the victims. The manager told us the only thing we could do was win it for them.”

“We play for England, for Manchester and for the people who died. We did it”, said Paul Pogba, the last

STOCKHOL
FINAL 2017

WAYNE ROONEY LIFTS THE TROPHY, FOLLOWING THE UEFA EUROPA LEAGUE FINAL MATCH AGAINST AJAX AT FRIENDS ARENA, 24TH MAY 2017

man out of the dressing room on that historic night.

With three trophies scalped from his first season at United, expectations were that Mourinho was going to herald in a new era in which Manchester United would fly high - perhaps not another Ferguson era, no one could touch him for achievement, but anything even approaching that would be great, thank you - the 2017-18 season saw the Reds get off to an eight-game run without loss, although they slipped from first place to 2nd in September, the week after a 2-2 draw against Stoke City. They also secured a fifth round place in the EFL Cup competition, and by December had finished top of their group in the UEFA Champions League group stage. It seemed as though the Mourinho magic was in plentiful supply. Lukaku was popping in goals regularly and Rashford was getting his share, too.

But appearances were cruelly deceptive. Unfortunately, the first signs of the engine stuttering were already apparent in the Premier League. Within three games from the 21st of October, the team suffered two defeats; against Huddersfield, 2-1, and against Chelsea, 1-0.

The lads recovered their equilibrium to win the next four games and stop the rot, and fortunately, their opponents - Manchester City was the exception - were not faring any better, so the Reds remained in 2nd place.

December 2017 and the fifth round of the EFL Cup; it brought the death of the first hope for silverware. A 2-1 loss against EFL Championship club Bristol City, despite some brilliant play by Lukaku and Rashford.

PAUL POGBA OF MANCHESTER UNITED CELEBRATES AS HE SCORES HIS TEAM'S SECOND GOAL DURING THE PREMIER LEAGUE MATCH BETWEEN MANCHESTER UNITED AND AFC BOURNEMOUTH AT OLD TRAFFORD

In the FA Cup run, Lukaku scored in every match except the semi-final as the Reds marched on into the final against Chelsea in May 2018. Admittedly, the opposition until the semi-final against Tottenham Hotspur should not have caused problems, anyway.

Tottenham were in scintillating mood as the semi-final game started, with Harry Kane's 20-yard drive, deflected behind for a corner, showing the team's intent. Their enterprise was rewarded after just 11 minutes with a goal by Alli. Tottenham kept up the pressure, and United soon had another narrow escape. But midway through the half, a perfect Pogba cross found Sanchez who headed home the equaliser.

With so little to separate them, the teams were wary of one another in the second half, but it was United who dared more and reaped the spoils for doing so. Appearing in the right place as if by

MARCUS RASHFORD CELEBRATES SCORING MANCHESTER UNITED'S THIRD GOAL WITH TEAMMATES CHRIS SMALLING AND TAHITH CHONG DURING THE UEFA CHAMPIONS LEAGUE ROUND OF 16 SECOND LEG MATCH AGAINST PARIS SAINT-GERMAIN, PARC DES PRINCES, MARCH 06 2019 IN PARIS, FRANCE

magic, Herrera put away the second goal after Sanchez and Lukaku had smoothly counter-attacked. A thrilling game and a deserved win.

Back in the Premier League, December was packed with seven matches; only three of them were won and one was lost, at home to Manchester City, though only by one goal.

On the 30th of December, the team slipped to 3rd place after a 0-0 draw against Southampton. They were back up to 2nd on January 1st with a win against Everton, 2-0, but although the next 14 games produced just two losses, Newcastle and Tottenham, the results dragged them further back behind the league leader, Manchester City. It was a similar story for the final six games; three won, one drawn and two lost. The extent of Mourinho's problem was seen in the points difference between the 1st and 2nd-placed teams; Manchester City were on 100 points; United were on 81.

When the season ended, there was no additional silverware gracing the club history. The UEFA Champions League competition ended abruptly for the Reds in February, knocked out by Sevilla, 2-1.

The last attempt at gaining a top prize was the FA Cup final against Chelsea. That dream floated away with Chelsea's lone winning goal. Hazard was downed by Jones, and the Chelsea goal from the spot went in on 22 minutes.

United then put on a display of thrilling football in the second half to try and salvage the game and came so close to doing so, keeping Chelsea on the back foot for most of the half. As the whistle sounded, though, they had been unable to penetrate the defence sufficiently, and the season was over, with Mourinho wondering what had gone wrong. The murmuring had started; the elite football world was not kind to managers without silverware.

Suffice to say it was not one of United's best seasons.

Mourinho's magic had deserted him; a glance at Paul Pogba's goalscoring record as top goalscorer for the following 2018-19 season suffices to see that all had not been well; 16 goals. In the 2014-15 season Wayne Rooney had scored 14 as top goalscorer and United had finished 4th, and in the 2012-13 season, the last time the club had won the Premiership, Robin van Persie had walloped in 30.

In May 2019, having lost all but 2 of their last 9

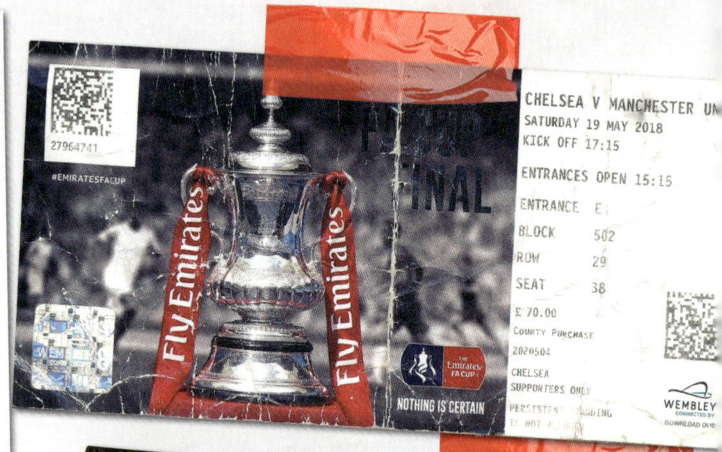

MARCUS RASHFORD OF MANCHESTER UNITED SCORES HIS SIDES FIRST GOAL DURING THE PREMIER LEAGUE MATCH BETWEEN MANCHESTER UNITED AND LIVERPOOL AT OLD TRAFFORD ON OCTOBER 20, 2019

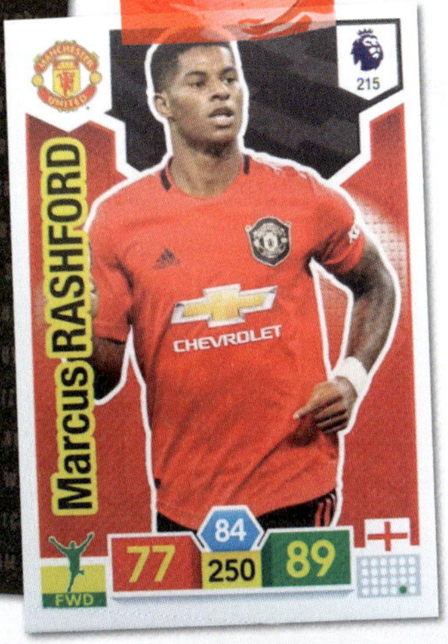

matches, United were 6th in the table, 32 points behind champions Manchester City. The FA Cup vanished when Wolverhampton Wanderers took the quarter-final 2-1. The EFA Champions League Cup vanished when Barcelona won both legs, 4-0 on aggregate.

None of the transfers in had made an impact of any note, neither Portuguese full-back Diogo Dalot, Brazilian Fred or midfielder Lee Grant.

The dismal 2019-20 season start ended with Mourinho's sacking in December after the fifth defeat, 1-3 against Liverpool.

Enter Ole Gunnar Solskjær as caretaker manager on December the 19th 2019.

The change in coaching methods produced results immediately. After 12 games without defeat, and now having worked their way up to fourth position, and despite his first loss, 1-0 to Arsenal, it appeared that Solskjær was in possession of some magic of his own to spread around. He was asked to stay on, accepted, saw his team beat Watford two days later - and then collapse to win just one game in the final six - which dropped them back down to sixth. Confusion and apprehension all around.

Nonetheless, Solskjær was still pulling the strings when the 2019-20 season hove into view. But he could now no longer call upon the steady skills of Antonio Valencia. The Ecuadorian right-back had called it a day in Manchester after 241 appearances, including captaining responsibilities, since 2009. Otherwise there were to be no great changes in the squad.

Alas, the new season proved to be as frustrating as the last one had been.

With the Covid pandemic running riot throughout the world, the team languished in 5th position in the league for much of the season, despite a blistering start with a 4-0 win against Chelsea, and had even dropped as low as 14th after just 2 wins in 9 outings!

United's FA Cup run was stopped by Chelsea, 3-1 in the semis. The same fate, at the feet of Manchester City again, in the EFL semis, 4-1 this time on aggregate. Their fate was repeated in the UEFA Europa League semi-final against Sevilla, only a Fernandes penalty to counter the Spanish team's 2 goals. And the Premier League? 3rd. With 66 points, still 33 behind the champions, Liverpool. Only 18 games won. How quickly hope falls off the shelf. Now Solskjær's head was on the block. Three seasons without a trophy was a serious record. Managers had departed for far less.

There were no notable new signings in the summer; the team staples Rashford, Fernandes, Luke Shaw, Harry Maguire and Wan-Bissaka would all clock up thirty and more league appearances apiece, Fernandes would claim the plaudits as top goalscorer with 28 hits. A lack of more top-notch players proved to be a weak point, for it left the manager with few options on the bench to alter match play and placed too much weight on Fernandes' shoulders. As a consequence, the team's performances would suffer if he were absent.

2020-21. This was not a season start designed to lighten hearts at Old Trafford. It produced just two wins from the first six games. Worse, three home defeats; to Crystal Palace, Tottenham Hotspur and Arsenal, at which point the team were in 15th place.

Solskjær had stated to the press: "We can't change the whole squad, but it's got to be one step at a time, and I've said all along I'm gonna be successful here".

Fans could do little more than hope that he was right.

By September's end, the EFL Cup run had produced two 3-0 wins, against Brighton and Luton. Everton were stiffer competition, but they, too, went down, 2-0. That was the end of EFL fun, though. United's nemesis of the moment, Manchester City, saw to that, winning 2-0 in the semi-final in December.

And then, Solskjær produced nothing less than a miracle in the Premier League. 13 games without a defeat, and with Manchester City not enjoying the absolute domination of the previous season, the Reds shot up to first place.

Who dared to deny that anything was possible after holding Manchester City to a draw? After the 6-2 thrashing of Leeds, both in December 2020?

After holding Leicester City, who were challenging hard for the top places, to a 2-2 draw in Leicester? Fernandes, Rashford and Cavani ran riot in front of the goal, Fernandes striking eight times during that 13-game unbeaten run, Rashford and Cavani taking four apiece.

Dubbed the 'War of the Roses', in the match against Leeds, the Reds displayed what they were capable of, producing stunning football that had Scott McTominay scoring twice within three minutes, his finishing nothing less than brilliant. He became the first Premier

MARCUS RASHFORD OF MANCHESTER UNITED CELEBRATES VICTORY AFTER THE PREMIER LEAGUE MATCH BETWEEN MANCHESTER CITY AND MANCHESTER UNITED AT ETIHAD STADIUM ON DECEMBER 07, 2019

HARRY MAGUIRE OF MANCHESTER UNITED TACKLES RAHEEM STERLING OF MANCHESTER CITY DURING THE CARABAO CUP SEMI-FINAL MATCH BETWEEN MANCHESTER CITY AND MANCHESTER UNITED AT ETIHAD STADIUM ON JANUARY 29, 2020

League player to score twice in the opening three minutes of a game. Not to be outdone, Bruno Fernandes was there at the end of a swift counter-attack with a low shot into the net, and Victor Lindelöf was soon on target, too, to make the lead 4-0. Just 37 minutes had passed. Heady stuff, even after Leeds managed to pull one back before the break.

In a less frenetic second half, James and Fernandes put the score on 6-1, with Leeds managing a second before leaving well and truly hammered at the final whistle.

Why, then, did the Premier League season begin to unravel at the end of January 2021 with the Reds at the top of the league? The FA Cup run started out well; Watford, Liverpool and West Ham were all dispensed with, one goal making the difference on each occasion; but it's results that matter.

The EFL Cup, on the other hand, was a breeze against Luton Town, 3-0, Brighton, 3-0 and Everton, 2-0.

That dreaded January saw Manchester City leave the semi-final heading into the final having beaten the Reds 2-0.

And the UEFA Champions League challenge had withered badly. United finished third in their group and were transferred to the Europa League competition. There, the lads did well through February, March and April, two of the most impressive scores being 4-0 against Real Sociedad in the round of 32 first leg and having progressed through Milan and Grenada, hammering Roma 6-2 in the semi-final. In that game, Bruno Fernandes took up Cavani's pass and scored a superb opener after just 9 minutes, and hope that United were on a roll was high. But the team allowed Roma to slot in two before half time. It seemed that what was being described as the "semi-final curse under Ole Gunnar Solskjaer", was raising its head again.

United came out fighting for the second half and within three minutes, Cavani had equalled the scores with a terrific first-time shot. United had to wait until the 64th minute for Cavani to get his second and they fought to keep that clear lead.

When Chris Smalling was penalised for what seemed like a fairly blameless tackle on Cavani, Fernandes was presented with his second goal of the night, from the penalty spot this time.

With Roma dispirited, the Reds powered on, and Pogba fired a header to make it 5 on the 75th minute. Greenwood put the icing on the cake with his contribution on the 86th after chasing another great Cavani pass to shoot in number 6. This was Manchester as the fans knew they could be, the first team since Real Madrid in the 1964 European Cup, to score six goals in a major European semi-final. Even the 3-2 loss to Roma in the second leg, Cavani netting another two, could not stop the northern lads from stepping out for the final against Villareal.

The rain-drenched final saw the Spaniards take the

EDINSON CAVANI OF MANCHESTER UNITED SCORES THEIR SIDE'S FIRST GOAL WHILST UNDER PRESSURE FROM BEN GODFREY OF EVERTON DURING THE CARABAO CUP QUARTER FINAL MATCH BETWEEN EVERTON AND MANCHESTER UNITED AT GOODISON PARK ON DECEMBER 23, 2020 IN LIVERPOOL, ENGLAND

lead after 29 minutes, United striking back on the 55th minute with a Cavani goal. But as the minutes ebbed away and extra time sapped the energy, the game became a tense, exhausting slog. It ended 1-1 and led to a harrowing penalty shoot out that finally saw United lose, 10-11. David De Gea missed the critical final penalty after 22 unstoppable spot-kicks.

It was a bitter blow. One that followed on the heels of a 3-1 loss to Leicester City in March in the FA Cup quarter-final game. The halo that had begun to form for Solskjær was already looking somewhat tarnished.

At least the lads were enjoying a 7-game unbeaten Premier League run at the time. True, that had been preceded by a sticky 8 games, which had produced just two wins. And true, one of those had been a blistering 9-0 defeat of Southampton. That score equalled the historic rout of Ipswich Town in 1995.

The Reds were absolutely scintillating and paid back the nasty tackle on McTominay by Jankewitz after just 77 seconds that could have ended far worse than it did. Once Wan-Bissaka had put away his first Old Trafford goal with a volley just 18 minutes in, the flood gates opened. David De Gea leapt like a demon to ensure the score stayed in United's favour, and an own goal by Bednarek came between hits by Rashford and then Cavani. Martial, McTominay and Fernandes' goals were rounded off by another Martial strike on 90, and James three minutes into injury time. A superb display that left fans breathless, yet wondering why such inconsistency in performances between matches.

There was still hope for the title, despite Liverpool breathing down their necks and a revitalised Chelsea. But the momentum faltered yet again that season with a 0-0 draw against Leeds in April. With just five games left to play, the steam left the United thrust. Only two of the games were won, with Leicester taking home a 2-1 advantage, Liverpool taking away a 2-4 win and Fulham sharing the points in a 1-1 draw in London.

The season finished with a Champions League qualification for second place; 74 points as opposed to Manchester City's 86.

United had suffered a fourth consecutive season without silverware. The disappointment was palpable, because this was the first time United had gone through this experience since 1981-82; not a record that a club of Manchester's calibre should be repeating.

But the seeds of hope for the future had been planted; second place in the league was a good springboard, because the quality of the team was evident on numerous occasions in all competitions. The top-notch players proved their worth; Rashford, Fred, Fernandes, Wan-Bissaka, and once the kinks in the system have been ironed out, the top prizes are tantalisingly within reach for 2021-22 and beyond.

MARCUS RASHFORD (L) AND MANCHESTER CITY'S BRAZILIAN MIDFIELDER FERNANDINHO (R) 'TAKE A KNEE' IN SUPPORT OF THE NO ROOM FOR RACISM CAMPAIGN AHEAD OF THE ENGLISH PREMIER LEAGUE MATCH BETWEEN MANCHESTER UNITED AND MANCHESTER CITY AT OLD TRAFFORD, DECEMBER 13, 2020

VILLARREAL'S SPANISH FORWARD GERARD MORENO (L) IS CLOSED DOWN BY MANCHESTER UNITED'S ENGLISH DEFENDER LUKE SHAW DURING THE UEFA EUROPA LEAGUE FINAL BETWEEN VILLARREAL CF AND MANCHESTER UNITED AT THE GDANSK STADIUM IN GDANSK ON MAY 26, 2021

MANCHESTER UNITED SUPPORTERS PROTEST AGAINST THE GLAZER OWNERSHIP OUTSIDE OLD TRAFFORD ON APRIL 24, 2021

MANCHESTER UNITED'S PLAYERS REACT TO THEIR DEFEAT IN THE UEFA EUROPA LEAGUE FINAL BETWEEN VILLARREAL CF AND MANCHESTER UNITED AT THE GDANSK STADIUM IN GDANSK ON MAY 26, 2021

PHOENIX

This was a historic season that marked United's 30 years in the Premier League, and hopes were high that some of the magic dust that fans had experienced under Sir Alex Ferguson might make reappearance.

Those hopes received a significant boost in August of 2021 when it was announced that after a 12-year sojourn abroad, Cristiano Ronaldo was returning to the United fold. It's hard to stay away, after all.

Yet, all hopes proved illusory, despite a cracking start to the season with a hat-trick by Fernandes in a 5-1 hammering of Leeds United to put United on top of the league. And so, undefeated for five games, the shock was mighty when the wheels came off as just one victory in eight games then left the team in eighth place.

By then, Ole Gunnar Solskjær – the first full-time manager since Frank O'Farrell to fail to bring home silverware for the club – had been severed from United by the hovering axe of dashed expectations, leaving Michael Carrick, the first-team coach to take over until interim manager Ralf Rangnick took up the reins eight days later.

The lads seemed to discover renewed energy and purpose with the change, finally bringing some sense of rhythm and intent to their play and delivering 14 games with just one defeat, at home to Wolverhampton Wanderers, who finished the season 10th.

United were carried through to March 2021 either on a ray of light that promised bright success or under a cloud and at risk of being extinguished, as the team struggled to lift themselves away from that seventh spot. Rivals Manchester City, Liverpool or Chelsea were the teams to be judged against, and a 4-2 win against a Leeds team that dropped to 18th at the end of the season was hardly a massive ray of hope, welcome as it was. Ronaldo, who was omnipresent throughout the season, rescued games and gladdened hearts, with a hat-trick against Tottenham Hotspur, for example, and another to rescue the game against Norwich City, giving a fleeting glimpse of what should have been normality for United fans. But Liverpool delivered a knockout blow in April in a 4-0 defeat that rammed home the obvious; something had to change or even the sixth spot the team had landed on five games before season end might finally seem like a distant dream.

CRISTIANO RONALDO APPEALS FOR A FOUL DURING THE UEFA CHAMPIONS LEAGUE GROUP F MATCH BETWEEN MANCHESTER UNITED AND ATALANTA AT OLD TRAFFORD ON OCTOBER 20, 2021

On 21st of April the revolving door turned again and in stepped Dutchman Erik ten Hag, fresh from managing Ajax, destined to assume the managerial mantel once the season ended. United was proving a tough gig for Ferguson's successors, but if Ten Hag could finally pull the rabbit out of the hat, the gratitude of fans would be assured for ever.

The Reds ended the season on 58 points, far behind winners Manchester City's 93, and thankful to still be in sixth place, an agonising fifth season without a trophy, an experience last endured between 1968/69 and 1973/74. United's worst season since 1989/90 ended with 57 goals conceded, the most since the 1978/79 season.

Every chance at silverware had vanished, and with a 4-0 scoreline, United suffered their worst-ever defeat against Brighton & Hove Albion and thus for the first time in in three years failed to qualify for the UEFA Champions League.

What had gone wrong? Many fingers pointed at Ronaldo, who came in for heavy criticism for not pressing high up the pitch, resting on his goal-scoring laurels and leaving the heavy lifting to his teammates. This attitude affected the team's cohesion and spirit of cooperation and eventually affected even the star's performances. Neither did his tantrums help the team to mould into an efficient, united fighting unit. The interim manager tactic had also failed to produce the longed-for results, so Ten Hag was now the man to try and pick up the pieces.

He would do so without Paul Pogba, who was leaving after 226 matches and 39 goals, and although one of the best in the world in his day, had struggled to find consistent form at United.

Ten Hag was facing a Herculean task; could he hold off the wolves long enough to build a team worthy of the United shirt?

For the parched United faithful, the answer was, thankfully, yes... although with slight reservations.

A forgettable season had passed into history, and before long, so had Ronaldo's second, failed, bite at Manchester glory. The striker's agent was already negotiating a transfer as the new season got underway, not a move designed to soothe troubled minds at the club, and by the time Ronaldo had been rejected by a

ERIK TEN HAG CELEBRATES → VICTORY AS JURGEN KLOPP LOOKS ON FOLLOWING THE PREMIER LEAGUE MATCH BETWEEN MANCHESTER UNITED AND LIVERPOOL FC AT OLD TRAFFORD ON AUGUST 22, 2022

RISING

CARABAO CUP FINAL 2023 WINNERS

MANCHESTER UNITED'S BRUNO FERNANDES AND HARRY MAGUIRE LIFT THE TROPHY TO CELEBRATE WITH REST OF THE TEAM AFTER THEIR VICTORY IN THE ENGLISH LEAGUE CUP FINAL AGAINST NEWCASTLE UNITED AT WEMBLEY STADIUM, FEBRUARY 26, 2023

swathe of clubs, Chelsea included, the atmosphere around him was turning toxic. Named captain, nonetheless, in November 2022, by the 22nd, his contract had been terminated. The agony for all sides was mercifully over.

Now Erik ten Hag could concentrate without distraction on the new members of his squad. Two midfielders would shore up the centre, Brazilian Casemiro, who although starting into his thirties would prove his worth by stabilising the centre and being sorely missed if he was absent, and Danish player Christian Eriksen, a man with impressive credentials. Into the defence came the Argentinian Lisandro Martínez, considered one of the best in the game and young winger Antony, whose debut goal arrived in September in a 3-1 home league victory over high-flyers Arsenal.

The lads set off on the campaign... and frightened the life out of everyone watching by losing the first two games, one against Brighton 2-1, with an own goal to agonise over, and then to Brentford... not quite as horrific a result as it seems, as Brentford became a middle of the table team... Well, all right, yes, it was as horrific as it seemed, because United landed in 20th place.

Then the joy. Four victories in a row, including against Liverpool, 2-1, and Arsenal, 3-1. Rashford was firing again scoring three in the two games and the club was up to fifth. Hope flared. And then it was crushed bitterly in a 3-6 defeat to Manchester City. But building a team to eradicate past disappointment takes time. Ten Hag held his nerve and managed to steady everyone else's nerves, too.

United began to find rhythm and purpose, an exercise in which Casemiro was outstanding as the team slowly began to carve out a reputation. Ronaldo scored his last goal in October and the manager then reshuffled to allow the front three more freedom. Without Ronaldo, Marcus Rashford was sent through the middle in penetrative breaks, leading high presses with Anthony Martial also working through the middle, but falling back to link with midfield more often, a change that proved effective. Bruno Fernandes, especially, was able to benefit from the free space to make runs from behind to beyond the defence. And the victorious results began to mount; 17 games with just two defeats told that a new chapter was starting for the club. The team moved into third position.

Rashford scored in 10 of those games, and as the season progressed he earned himself the accolade of European player enjoying the best form.

One of the most exciting and satisfying games came in January 2023 against a surging Manchester City. If the Manchester men in blue had thought to repeat their success of earlier, they were mistaken. United absorbed the early City pressure, only to fall victim to a Grealish goal on the hour. Undaunted, in fact incensed, United worked hard and were rewarded when Fernandes equalised. Now showing what they were capable of, the team pressed on and that man Rashford hit gold on the 82nd minute to seal a memorable comeback win.

And suddenly, there was it was, the moment that had everyone longed for. United held up silverware for the first time since the Europa League in 2017. The team had made it to the EFL final in February against Newcastle United, and did more than hold off the doggedly persistent Magpies; they put in two goals courtesy of dashing duo Casemiro and Rashford. A six-year drought had come to an end.

But then the wobbles returned; Liverpool put in a devastating 7-0 victory, best erased from memory, and two more games passed in a draw and defeat.

As the end-spurt towards the final games began, however, United recovered and remained glued to the fourth spot, where they needed just one point with two league games left, in order to qualify for the Champions League. And, there was to be a season thriller no less – the FA Cup Final against Manchester City. What a difference a year makes!

So it would be Chelsea up first and then Fulham to chase that point, both teams lounging in the middle of the table.

The 25th May 2023 rolled around; with so much at stake the optimistic tension in the air at Old Trafford could have been cut with a knife. So it was almost an anti-climax, the mastery that United brought to the match, sending in wave after wave of attacks that could so easily have resulted in a slaughter instead of a rout. As it was, Casemiro laid down the statement of intent after just six minutes with a header from close range. Although Chelsea managed to hang on until injury time in the first half, Martial increased the lead slotting the ball into an empty net.

With United dominating play again in the second half, it was just a matter of time before they put the match beyond the Londoners' reach and that happened on the 73rd minute thanks to a penalty from Fernandes, and number four went in after Rashford had danced around the Chelsea keeper five minutes later.

Ten Hag had reason to be pleased; United were back in Europe, where they belong, as Ten Hag rightfully emphasised. So the team could relax for the final match of the season against Fulham, because Ten Hag's magic had also brought the Reds back to Wembley for the FA Cup final. What a magnificent triumph that would be, especially against the Blues from across the city; but notwithstanding the result of that game, what a triumphant night this 25th of May had been for Erik ten Hag and his boys.

The final league match of the season, on the 28th of May, pitted United against Fulham in a game that brought United their fourth consecutive win with Sancho and Fernandes making it 2-1 to bring to an end a highly successful campaign in which Ten Hag had revived the

BRUNO FERNANDES SCORES FROM THE PENALTY SPOT DURING THE EMIRATES FA CUP FINAL BETWEEN MANCHESTER CITY AND MANCHESTER UNITED AT WEMBLEY STADIUM ON JUNE 03, 2023

club's fortunes in spectacular style and the club finished in third place in the Premier League.

So the team headed to Wembley for the FA Cup final with a justified confidence that they could hold their own against Manchester City. It was a vast shower of cold water, therefore, when Ilkay Gündogan fired in a volley, the fastest-ever in an FA Cup final, after just 13 seconds. United's lapse of concentration had allowed him too much space and United were 1-0 down.

It is, however, a sign of the renewed personal determination in the team that they did not hang their heads and submit to what might have been a fierce defeat from that point on.

The reward for keeping their heads came in the form of a penalty from a, yes, somewhat fortunate handball call, before a United attack fizzled out. When Fernandes stepped up and wrong-footed the City keeper, Ortega, United were back on level pegging.

Only for United to commit the same mistake again and allow Gündogan to slip unguarded on the edge of the box. And as a cross floated over to him, he volleyed for a second time. The ball bounced through three defenders and into the net just avoiding the fingertips of the diving De Gea.

United created only a few clear-cut attempts at goal, but seemed rejuvenated in the second half with substitute Alejandro Garnacho's shot almost bringing United back into the game, as did a cracker from Rashford and a bouncing ball that came down on top of the City bar. With a City goal disallowed for offside, the score stayed 2-1 at the final whistle. The team had held their own against their Manchester rivals and could be proud that they had fought their way up the league and the to the FA Cup final, and for refusing to give in, preventing City from looking their best by doing so.

Ten Hag has reasons to be optimistic, but pepper that optimism with caution, and possesses an encouragingly steely determination to fight for the top awards. "We are still in a journey," he mused, "we think we are in the right direction but it can always be better. Because good is not good enough." Words to warm the hearts of Manchester fans everywhere.

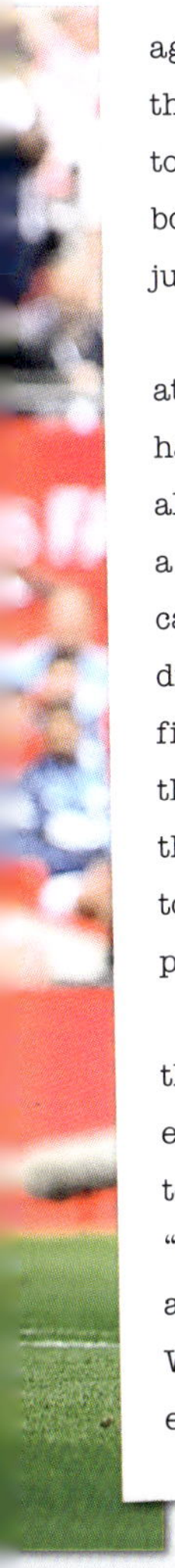

And to consolidate the excellent revamped United, Ten Hag went on the prowl, searching for a centre-forward, a box-to-box midfielder and a new right-back to beef up his squad. Exciting times had returned to Old Trafford and fans could dream again.

In what was described as play that was "outstanding and clinical in the 2022/23 campaign," David de Gea had been nothing short of "brilliant", Casemiro had "changed the dynamics of the midfield", and who else but Marcus Rashford deserved the prize for best player of 2023.

MANCHESTER UNITED. THE NAME IS SYNONYMOUS WITH SCINTILLATING STAR PLAYERS, STUNNING VICTORIES AND THE TOP AWARDS AT HOME AND ABROAD. IT IS A CLUB THAT HAS PERSEVERED IN THE FACE OF PROFESSIONAL AND PERSONAL ADVERSITY AND EMERGED TO THRILL ITS SUPPORTERS WITH FOOTBALL THAT CAN TAKE YOUR BREATH AWAY. THERE WILL ALWAYS BE HIGHS AND LOWS, EXCITEMENT AND DISAPPOINTMENT IN FOOTBALL, BUT MANCHESTER UNITED WILL NEVER BE FAR FROM THE THICK OF THE ACTION AND WILL FIGHT FOR THE TOP HONOURS EVERY INCH OF THE WAY AS THEY HAVE ALWAYS DONE, SPURRED ON BY LOYAL FANS WHO WILL RAISE THE LADS IN RED TO THE TOP OF THEIR GAME, EVERY TIME THEY RUN ONTO THE FIELD OF PLAY.

THE PLAYERS

A LIST OF THE MOST FAMOUS PLAYERS MUST INEVITABLY BE SHORTER THAN IT SHOULD BE AND WILL ALWAYS BE DISPUTED BY THE SUPPORTERS OF ONE PLAYER OR ANOTHER BUT HERE ARE SOME OF THOSE WHO MUST GRACE EVERY LIST.

BILLY MEREDITH

1906-1921

Born in northern Wales on 30 July 1874 and died on 19 April 1958.

Whilst playing for Manchester City in the 1904/05 season he was found guilty of bribing an opposition player to lose and given an 18-month ban from playing for the club. He moved to Manchester United where he made his debut on 1st January 1907 against Aston Villa. Meredith won the league title with United in 1908 and 1911 and the FA Cup in 1909.

In 1908 he played in all the league matches except one, making 37 appearances and scoring 10 goals as the Red Devils won their first ever First Division championship.

Meredith was a superb provider of goals showing great speed, and the ultimate team leader. He played his last match for United on 7th May 1921 when he was almost 48 years old having made 339 appearances and scoring 129 goals. He then left United for Manchester City and played his last professional match when he was almost 50. He gained 48 caps for Wales scoring 11 goals.

DUNCAN EDWARDS

1952-1958

He was born on the 1st October 1936 and died of kidney failure following the Munich Air Disaster, on the 21st February 1958. Bobby Moore said he was like the Rock of Gibraltar as a defender and "dynamic coming forward". He was nicknamed "The Tank" and was ranked amongst the toughest players of all time. His professional career lasted less than five years but he helped United to win two Football League Championships and reach the European Cup semi-finals.

His debut came against Scotland on the 2nd April 1955 at the age of 18 years and 183 days, England's youngest debutant since WWII.

His final match for United was against Red Star Belgrade in a 3-3 away draw.

Edwards played 151 league games scoring 21 goals in all competitions. Edward's power and the timing of his tackles made him notorious and he had the rare ability to pass and shoot equally well with both feet. He was well known for tremendous runs up the pitch and heading the ball, and powerful long-range shots were also in his armoury.

BOBBY CHARLTON

1954-1973

Charlton was born on the 11th October 1937 in Ashington in Northumberland. His first match for United was in October 1956 against Charlton Athletic when the teenage Charlton scored twice in the 4-2 win. He became one of Busby's Babes. Charlton went on to play 14 times for United in his first season, striking a total of 12 goals in all competitions. In a 5-1 away win over Charlton Athletic again, in February, he scored a hat-trick and United won the League championship.

Even Charlton could not command a permanent place in the 1957/58 team as it was so good and did not play for the first ten matches. He was, however, in the team that played twice against Red Star Belgrade in the European Cup and was in Yugoslavia for the 3-3 draw against them on the 5th February 1958 when he scored twice.

The team plane crashed at Munich airport on the way home and Charlton was thrown 40 yards away from the wreckage and survived. With only minor injuries he left hospital one week later. He was just 20 years old.

Matt Busby rebuilt his side and Charlton was now a key player. He was called up to the England squad in 1959 at the age of 21. A thumping volley goal against Scotland enhanced his reputation and after 2 goals in his second England game he became indispensable. He became known as a scorer of great goals and a great goal scorer and had scored two hat-tricks for England by 1961 and by 1962 he had scored 25 goals in just 38 appearances for England. Charlton became captain of the United side. In the FA Cup final of 1963, he finally gained a winners' medal. It was his third final and United beat Leicester City 3-1. Two league championships within three seasons, in 1963 and 1965 and Charlton was at the peak of his form. Busby made use of him as a left-winger, inside-forward, centre-forward and midfielder. He had many skills; he was tactically aware and his powerful shooting abilities and gracious manner on and off the field made him one of the truly great players. In the classic 1966 World Cup Final against Germany (Charlton had scored two in the semi-final against Portugal) he was set against a young Franz Beckenbauer and the two marked each other so tightly that Charlton had a relatively quiet game. England won 4-2 after extra time. He was named European Footballer of the Year and English Football Writer's Association Player of the Year.

Another milestone was winning the European Championship in 1968 against Benfica when Charlton scored two of the goals in the 4-1 United victory.

With United slipping in the league, 1969 brought Charlton an OBE for services to football. He also won his 100th England cap on the 21st April 1970 against Northern Ireland, having been made captain by Alf Ramsey for the game. He scored his 48th goal for his country.

The 49th would be his final goal and it followed a month later in a 4-0 win over Colombia during a World Cup warm-up match.

Charlton left the Club in 1973 having scored 249 goals in 758 appearances and won 106 England caps. He spent time at Preston North End, Waterford in Ireland and Wigan. He became a United director in 1984 by which time he was also a CBE as well. He was knighted in 1994 for services to football. In 2008 he was given the BBC Sports Personality of the Year Lifetime Achievement Award.

NORBERT "NOBBY" STILES 1960-1971

Born on 18th May 1942 in Manchester, England he made his debut for Manchester United on 1st October 1960 against Bolton Wanderers. Stiles was a permanent member of the team for the next 8 seasons unless injury prevented him from playing. He won two league championship medals in 1965 and 1967 and was a crucial member of the England team that won the World Cup in 1966. He was a fearless tackler and again played a crucial role in helping United to win the European Cup in 1968 with his tight marking of Benfica's Eusebio. He was very successful in midfield shutting down skilled opponents and skilfully gaining ball possession.

Stiles won 28 England caps and scored one goal. He spent 11 years at Old Trafford and made 311 appearances for the team. He is only one of three Englishmen to have won both the World Cup and the European Cup.

He then left Manchester for Preston North End, Vancouver and West Bromwich Albion. He was awarded the MBE in 2000.

DENIS LAW

1960-1971

Law was born in Aberdeen, Scotland on the 24th February 1940 and made his debut against West Bromwich Albion on the 18th August 1962 when he scored after just 7 minutes. He was the ultimate goal scorer and United fans called him "the King".

Law moved to Manchester in July 1962 when the team was being rebuilt after Munich and in his first season he scored 29 goals. The following year George Best arrived and Law, Best and Charlton became the "Holy Trinity" providing an era of uniquely exciting football. He slammed in another 39 goals in the 1964/65 season but received a knee injury that would cause him trouble for the rest of his career. He was also named European Footballer of the Year and Manchester United won their first league title since Munich. With 28 league goals that season, Law became the First Division's top scorer.

When he won the league with United in 1966/67 Law was an international star and he went on to win 55 caps for Scotland with a tally of 30 goals. But his knee injury kept him out of the famous United European Cup win in 1968. He was in hospital for an operation. Law often claimed that referees were tougher on him because he had complained about the goading that one of them had given him earlier in his career. He spent two months on suspension in one year alone.

Injury meant that he missed almost all of the 1969/70 season. Law never regained the form of his earlier years and his knee trouble reduced the number of matches he played and the goals he scored.

After 11 years at the club, Law was given a free transfer by Tommy Docherty, the man Law had recommended for manager. Law had scored a total of 237 goals in 404 games in all competitions, and picked up two league title medals and an FA Cup winner's medal.

Law moved to Manchester City and scored against his former mates the season they were relegated and left the field with his head down thinking he had helped sink his former club. The 2-1 victory against Oldham Athletic at Maine Road on the 6th August 1974 was his last professional game. He became a TV commentator.

GEORGE BEST 1963-1974

George Best was a shy young teenager kicking balls on the tough Cregagh Estate in Belfast until he was spotted by Bob Bishop the Manchester United scout. "Boss, I think I've found a genius" Bishop told Busby. Best was 15 years old. He went to Manchester but then returned to Belfast suffering from home sickness but he eventually signed for the club on his 17th birthday.

George Best was born in East Belfast on 22nd May 1946. His unique career began on the 14th September 1963 against West Bromwich Albion at Old Trafford. Busby allowed him onto the field for 26 matches that first season when he scored 6 goals. After that he was the magician of Manchester, his performances simply breathtaking in their audacity and skill.

Best, Denis Law and Bobby Charlton formed what was probably the greatest football trio of all time. With them, Best helped United win the league championship in his second season.

Best's wild celebrity status truly took off when at the age of twenty, "the fifth Beatle", as the Portuguese press were now calling him, fired in two goals against Benfica in the European Cup quarter finals in the 1965/66 season. He became the first showbiz footballer, his long hair, good looks and blazing talent making him a favourite on and off the field. By the end of that football year, Best was already a sporting legend.

In the 1966/67 season, United and Best won the league title with Best scoring ten goals. The following year was one of the best ever for the club. Best was outstanding and scored 32 goals. He was in a class of his own. Playing magnificently in all games, he helped steer the club towards the European Cup Final against Benfica and with typical coolness scored the second goal in the 4-1 victory. It was inevitable that he would be crowned as European Footballer of the Year and Player of the Year by the English football press.

Who could have dreamed that he had reached the pinnacle and that from now on he would slide downhill. Best was getting over 1,000 fan mail letters a week. He opened two nightclubs in Manchester and was beginning to have problems as a womaniser, gambler and alcoholic.

Busby, father figure to Best, retired and passed on the only advice he could about the wayward star. "Let him alone. Don't try to coach him." Nothing helped. He had confrontations with new managers and once vanished to Majorca threatening to quit. Best returned. Although capable of bursts of genius, with two mediocre seasons and Manchester heading down to Division Two, Best finally scored his last goal for United in a 3-2 home league defeat against Coventry City on 15 December 1973. He left United for good after his last match, on 2nd January 1974. He was only 27 and was never to play as well again.

Best had appeared for United 470 times in all competitions between 1963 and 1974. He had scored 179 goals, which included six in one game against Northampton Town of the fourth division. This performance was ranked as 26th in the 100 greatest sporting moments in 2002. For six seasons he was at the top of the list of top scorer's at the club and was top scorer in the First Division during the 1967-68 season. He was also capped 37 times for Northern Ireland for whom he scored nine goals.

For the next ten years he moved about constantly whilst his physical decline continued. He played for clubs from Dunstable Town to South Africa, taking in Ireland and Australia whilst his career headed for the buffers.

With several marriages behind him, drunken appearances on TV, a gaol sentence and a kidney transplant, he died on the 25th November 2005.

Amongst the glorious achievements, one goal that was officially not a goal at all perhaps sums up the cheeky football genius that was George Best.

On 15th May 1971, at Windsor Park playing for Northern Ireland against England, Best was down with the England keeper Gordon Banks. Banks let go of the ball to kick it downfield when Best got a foot to it. The ball arced upwards towards the open goal and Best was first to get there heading the ball into the empty goal. Referee Alistair Mackenzie disallowed the goal, wrongly. It was typically audacious, fearless George Best skill.

THE WONDERFUL WORLD OF
SOCCER STARS IN ACTION
"PICTURE STAMP ALBUM"
England First Division
1969-1970
2'6

BRYAN ROBSON

1981-1994

Born on 11th January 1957, he made his debut for United on the 7th October 1981 against Tottenham. In his first season for the club he scored five times in 32 appearances. He scored his first goal for United on the 7th November 1981 in a 5-1 win against Sunderland. He also scored a goal after just 20 seconds against France in 1982, a record that stood for 20 years.

The following season, Robson was United's captain and became the longest serving captain in the club's history. He scored twice in the FA Cup victory against Brighton and Hove Albion that season and typically allowed another player to convert a penalty instead of going for a hat-trick.

He became a Manchester United hero when, in what many think was his finest hour, he scored twice in leading United's astonishing fight back against Barcelona in the European Cup Winners' Cup.

He was awarded an OBE in 1990 for services to football, taking the FA Cup trophy with United the same year. The first trophy since Atkinson was sacked in 1986. Robson became the first United captain to win the cup three times. Robson had been fighting injury once again that season, making just 20 league appearances.

Robson was still a regular choice for United during the 1991/92 season but made just 14 league appearances. During that season he appeared for England for the 90th and last time. Robson lifted another Premiership championship medal in 1993/94, and scored the last of his 99 goals for the club, one of their four goals in the FA Cup semi-final victory against Oldham. He was dropped from the squad for the FA Cup final, which manager Alex Ferguson admitted was one of the hardest decisions of his career. His last appearance for the Reds came on the 8th May 1994. United drew 0-0 at home against Coventry City. Robson played 461 times for United in all competitions, being widely considered to be one of the finest players ever to wear the red shirt.

RYAN GIGGS

1987-2014

Born on the 29th November 1973 in Wales. Giggs received an offer for a professional contract with United on his 17th birthday, the 29th November 1990. Giggs' League debut was against Everton at Old Trafford on the 2nd March 1991. He was a substitute for the injured full-back Denis Irwin. Giggs was credited with his first ever goal in a 1-0 win in the derby with Manchester City on the 4th May 1991 his first full game, although it seemed to be an own goal by Colin Hendry.

At the start of the 1992/93 season, Giggs had become first choice for the left wing position. He and Steve McManaman were recognised as English football's two best emerging young wingers. Giggs and United went on to win the league title, the first win for 26 years.

In the 1993-94 season, Giggs became the first player in history to win two consecutive PFA Young Player of the Year awards winning the league and cup double with United. Like Charlton, Giggs was a scorer of great goals, and many were shortlisted for various awards. Amongst his best were the ones scored against QPR in 1993, Tottenham in 1994, Everton in 1995, Coventry in 1996, and Arsenal in the 1999 FA Cup semi-final after a solo run.

His 4th Premier League medal arrived in the 1996/97 season. The following season he gained his Champions League winner's medal. Injuries and Ferguson's reluctance to overuse his star player had limited the number of Giggs' appearances and they fell from a high of 50 in the first seasons. Giggs set up the equalising goal in the 1999 UEFA Champions League Final putting United en route to the treble.

In May 2002, Giggs became United's longest serving player. He became a vital fulcrum to the club and he excelled in the four years that followed the treble of 1999. For three of the next four seasons United were Premier League Champions. Giggs celebrated his 10 years at the club in 2001-02. One year later, in autumn 2002, he scored his 100th career goal at Stamford Bridge.

On the 22nd May 2004, he became one of only two players to win the FA Cup trophy four times playing for Manchester United. In September 2004 he became the third player to play 600 games for United and in 2005 he was inducted into the English Football Hall of Fame in recognition of his contribution to the English game. In 2007 he won his 9th league medal, a record.

On the 12th September 2009, Giggs made his 700th appearance for United and scored his 150th goal. On the 28th November that year he scored his 100th league goal scoring the final goal against Portsmouth in a 4-1 victory, becoming only the 17th player to reach the target in the Premier League.

Giggs became BBC Sports Personality of the Year in 2009, and on the 31st December 2009, he was named the Manchester United Player of the Decade. Giggs scored his first ever league penalties on the 24th April 2010 netting two against Tottenham in a 3-1 home win.

In 2010/11 he won his 12th League winner's medal and is United's most decorated player.

PETER SCHMEICHEL

1991-1999

Born in Denmark on the 18th November 1963. The "Great Dane" was 6' 3" tall and made his debut for United aged 27 on the 17th August 1991 against Notts County.

Schmeichel went on to win five FA Premier League titles, three FA Cups, one League Cup, four Charity Shields and the UEFA Champions League with United. Manchester United won the Football League Cup for the first time in the club's history in his first season and Schmeichel was elected "The World's Best Goalkeeper 1992".

United won the Premier League in the 1992/93 season, with Schmeichel keeping his goal empty 22 times which helped United win the Premier League championship after 26 years. Schmeichel became "The World's Best Goalkeeper" again in 1993.

After a massive row in January 1994 between Schmeichel and Ferguson, Schmeichel "said the most horrible things", and was sacked by Ferguson. Schmeichel gave an apology to the other players that Ferguson overheard and he reinstated Schmeichel. Schmeichel and United won the Premier League championship again that season.

Even though he was a goalkeeper, he would often go into the attack and scored a goal for Man United, in a 1995 UEFA Cup match in the last minutes of the game.

When he witnessed a collision that left David Busst of Coventry with a compound fracture of the leg and the bone pierced through the skin leaving blood on the pitch, Schmeichel, had to receive counselling. In 1999, Schmeichel ended his Manchester United career winning the treble with United in the same season. He saved a penalty in the FA Cup semi-final against Arsenal that year and captained United in the UEFA Champions League final in May 1999. Against Bayern Munich Schmeichel ran into the attack and United scored an equalising goal. United won 2-1 and Schmeichel's United career ended on a high note.

Schmeichel was UEFA Goalkeeper of the Year four times and won 129 caps for Denmark before he retired in 2003; he had also played for Sporting Lisbon, Aston Villa and Manchester City.

ERIC CANTONA

1992-1997

Eric Daniel Pierre Cantona was born in Marseille in France in 1966, starting his career with Manchester United on 27th November 1992 coming from league champions Leeds United. His fiery temper was already a problem before he reached United and he had, in fact, retired from football after he had thrown the ball at the referee in a French match and called the hearing committee "Idiots." He was persuaded to restart his career away from France.

Cantona made his league debut for Manchester as a substitute in the game against Manchester City on 6th December 1992. (He had already played in red in a friendly match against Benfica in Lisbon to celebrate Eusebio's 50th birthday) His nine goals that season propelled United to another league championship title the first for 26 years. He became the first player to win the title in consecutive seasons with different clubs.

In the 1993/94 season he wore the no. 7 shirt drawing comparisons with George Best and had never played better as United went on to win their first league and cup double. Cantona scored 26 goals in total, 2 in the FA Cup Final 3-1 win against Aston Villa. He was voted Professional Footballers' Association Player of the Year.

His temper continued to get the better of him. He was sent off for a shouting match with the referee in the Champions League and shown the red card twice for stamping on opponents.

Then, in the 1994/95 season he committed an act that would blacken the reputation of football. By January the 22nd 1965 with 12 goals to his credit, Cantona was earning his right to the title of the fans' "King Cantona".

On the 25th, Cantona kicked a Crystal Place defender who had pulled his shirt; he was shown the red card. Walking towards the tunnel, Cantona threw a "kung-fu"-style kick at Crystal Palace fan Matthew Simmons and then attacked with a rain of punches. Cantona was arrested, convicted for assault and sent to prison for two weeks. The appeal court turned his conviction into 120 hours of community service.

Cantona was suspended by Manchester United for the remaining four months of the season and he was fined £20,000.

The FA with FIFA agreement then handed out an eight-month, world-wide ban and he was fined another £10,000 with FA Chief Executive Graham Kelly calling the attack ". . a stain on our game."

His famous quote "When the seagulls follow the trawler, it's because they think sardines will be thrown into the sea." implied, as he later confirmed, that he was not perturbed by what he had done and that such actions were expected of him or at the very least, hoped for.

When Cantona returned for the 1995/96 season, he was not in the top condition he had been before the ban. But as he improved, so did United, and they went on to their second league title. Cantona scored nine of the goals in a run of 13 wins in 15 games. His most glorious moment was in the

FA Cup final. He had been made captain for the match and struck the only goal in the 86th minute to give United the trophy. He became the first player from outside Britain to be captain in an FA Cup-winning side. Manchester United became the first team to win "the double" twice.

Cantona entered his final season with United, as their captain. He led them to victory in the league again in 1996/97, when he was top goal scorer with 15 goals.

He then surprised everyone by announcing that he was retiring. He was 30 years old.

Cantona had scored 82 goals in 185 appearances for the club. With United he had won four league titles in five years, which meant he had won six in seven years including those with Leeds United and Marseille. In 2003 he collected the Overseas Player of the Decade Award.

"I loved the game" he remarked, "but I no longer had the passion to go to bed early, not to go out with my friends, not to drink, and not to do a lot of other things, the things I like in life."

HE WAS AN OUTSTANDING TALENT, A TRUE MANCHESTER UNITED MAVERICK.

ROY KEANE

1993-2005

Born in Cork in the Irish Republic on the 10th August 1971. He began his career at Manchester United on the 7th August 1993 against Arsenal.

Keane was noted for his aggressive and highly competitive style and was a dominating central-midfielder. His first red card came in a 2-0 win in an FA Cup semi-final replay against Crystal Palace for stamping and he was suspended for three matches with a fine of £5,000. Keane earned eleven red cards in his United career, his fiery temper causing indiscipline on the field. The 1996/97 season saw Keane in and out of the side owing to a series of knee injuries and suspensions. He became captain of United from 1997 until his departure in 2005. He missed most of his first season as captain due to a cruciate ligament injury. The following year 1998/99 United netted the treble. In 2000 his talent earned him Player of the Year. Keane helped United achieve a sustained period of success in more than 12 years at the club.

In the 2001 Manchester derby game, he was sent off for a blatant knee-high foul on the Norwegian Alf-Inge Håland in what seemed to many to be an act of revenge. In August 2002, he said in his autobiography that he intended "to hurt" the Norwegian:

Following this confession to a premeditated assault, the FA had no choice but to charge Keane with bringing the game into disrepute and he received another ban for a further five matches and was fined £150,000. In August 2002 Ferguson fined him £150,000 and suspended him for three matches for elbowing a Sunderland player.

After a hip operation, Keane became more restrained on the field, avoided disputes and confrontations with other players, but Keane was as tenacious as ever and led the team to another league title in May 2003. His 50th goal for Manchester United came on the 5th February 2005 against Birmingham City.

Keane left Manchester United by mutual consent on the 18th November 2005. He had made 458 appearances for the club and scored 51 goals and had led United to 9 major titles, making him the most successful captain in the club's history. He spent a season at Celtic before announcing his retirement from playing on 12th June 2006.

DAVID BECKHAM

1993-2003

Born on the 2nd May 1975 in Leytonstone, East London he made his debut for United on the 23rd September 1992 against Brighton and Hove Albion. He made 356 appearances for the club and scored 85 goals. He signed schoolboy forms with United on his 14th Birthday and made his first-team debut in 1992 when he was 17. He was loaned out to Preston North End to gain experience and in 1995/96 helped United to win a second Premiership-FA Cup double. He won the FA Cup twice and the Premier League title six times with United. His incredible goal chipped from 60 yards brought him national attention the following season.

Beckham quickly established himself as United's right-sided midfielder and scored the goal that helped United to a league title in the 1998/99 season.

In his UEFA Champions League debut on the 7th December 1994, Beckham scored a goal in a 4-0 victory at home to Galatasaray.

His England debut came on the 1st September 1996, when he was 21 years old. From the 15th November 2000 until the FIFA World Cup finals in 2012 he was captain of the side and played 58 times. His one hundredth cap was earned against France on the 26th March 2008.

Beckham was a crucial player when United won a third successive league title in 2000/01 scoring nine goals during the season in the Premier League. The 2001/02 season was perhaps Beckham's best with United. He struck 11 goals in 28 league games, with a total of 16 goals in 42 games in all competitions, the greatest number in his career. He left Manchester United and signed for Real Madrid in 2003, the transfer being completed on the 1st July and he received the OBE for services to football on the 13th June that year.

In 2004 Beckham was the world's highest-paid footballer, taking salary and advertising deals into account, and also the first British footballer to play in 100 Champions League matches.

Further appearances with Real Madrid, LA Galaxy and AC Milan followed his departure from United.

TEDDY SHERINGHAM

1997-2001

Born on the 2nd of April 1966, England, he made his debut for Manchester United on 10th August 1997 against Tottenham Hotspur.

His first season with United got off to a slow start. He scored 14 goals in all competitions. In that first season, his relationship with fellow striker Andy Cole turned sour and they never spoke again. The following season, Dwight Yorke was signed and Sheringham's chances of appearing in the first team were reduced.

Sheringham has won almost every domestic honour available and was voted Player of the Year by both the Professional Footballers' Association and the Football Writers' Association. He left United in 2001 and returned to Tottenham Hotspur. His most successful season was in 1998/99 when he won the Treble with Manchester United. In 1999, he scored the equalizer and provided the assist for United's winning goal against Bayern Munich in the UEFA Champions League final. Sheringham was also an England international being capped 51 times scoring 11 goals. Sheringham was awarded an MBE in June 2007. He retired from competitive football in 2008 at the age of 42 years after a career that had lasted 25 years.

PAUL SCHOLES

1994-2013

Born in Salford, England, on 16th November 1974, Scholes made his United debut on the 21st September 1994 against Port Vale.

Scholes came into his own in the 1995/96 season as a support striker to Andy Cole and he scored 14 goals that season in all competitions, winning the Premiership and the FA Cup with the team. The next season he collected a league winner's medal. He also played a crucial role in the 1998/99 season when United won the Double.

One of Scholes' invaluable attributes is his ability to score important goals in big games. This happened in 2009/10 when he scored against Milan to give the Red Devils their first ever away win against the Rossoneri.

He won 13 FA Cup, 2 UEFA Champions League and 10 Premier League winner's medals. He was considered by many to be one of the best midfielders of his generation but he marred his record with 120 bookings during his career when he was sent off 10 times.

Scholes made 697 appearances for United before announcing his retirement on 31st May 2011 and then returning to play the following season.

RUUD VAN NISTELROOY

2001-2006

Born the 1st July 1976 in Holland, van Nistelrooy is the second-highest goalscorer in the Champions League with 60 goals. He is a three-time Champions League top scorer, as well as a top scorer in three different European domestic leagues. During his first season with United, 2001/02, van Nistelrooy scored 23 goals in 32 league games and became PFA Players' Player of the Year.

He was successful with United and won the Premier League, FA Cup, League Cup and FA Community Shield and also the Sir Matt Busby Player of the Year award twice. Van Nistelrooy struck 150 goals in just 219 games for United and was their all-time European record goalscorer. He departed for Real Madrid in 2006 and then for Hamburg. On the 14th May 2012 he announced his retirement from football.

He made 220 appearances for United. He scored 38 goals to become the club's all-time European top goalscorer.

CRISTIANO RONALDO

2003-2009 & 2021-2022

Born on the 5th February 1985 in Portugal. Wearing the no. 7 shirt, he made his debut for United on 16th August 2003 as a 60th-minute substitute against Bolton Wanderers in a 4-0 home victory. A 3-0 win over Portsmouth on the 1st November 2003 gave him his first goal for the club. He scored the first goal in United's 3-0 Victory in the FA Cup final over Millwall.

On the 29th October 2005 he scored United's 1000th Premier League goal when United lost 4-1 to Middlesborough. Ronaldo scored ten goals in all competitions. He was voted FIFPro Special Young Player of the Year in 2005. On the 14th January 2006 he was sent off when he kicked Andrew Cole in a match against Manchester City. But he won his second trophy in the Football League Cup final against Wigan Athletic when he scored the third goal.

Ronaldo then began to shine. He scored 91 goals in the next three seasons helping United to win eight trophies including three premiership titles. He formed an effective partnership on the field with Wayne Rooney. Ronaldo's first hat trick for Manchester United came on the 12th January 2008 in a 6-0 win against Newcastle United at Old Trafford.

In 2007 he was the first player to win all four main PFA and FWA awards and was FWA Footballer of the Year. In 2008, he won the Ballon d'Or, the first United player since George Best to do so. In 2008 and 2011 he was awarded the European Golden Shoe. In 2008, he also won three of the four main PFA and FWA trophies. The same year he became FIFPro Special Young Player of the Year, World Soccer Player of the Year, Onze d'Or and FIFA World Player of the Year and FWA Footballer of the Year for the second time. In 2009, Ronaldo was the inaugural winner of the FIFA Puskás Award.

Ronaldo captained United for the first time on the 19th March 2008 with a home win over Bolton, when he scored both goals in the 2-0 victory. He finished that season with a career high of 42 goals in all competitions. He was named best forward in the Champions League and was the top goal scorer in that league.

On 11th June, Manchester United accepted an unconditional offer of £80 million from Real Madrid for Ronaldo. After 292 appearances and 118 goals Ronaldo left United for Real Madrid.

Ronaldo made a hero's return to the club in 2021, hoping to fix their striker woes present since the departure of Rooney. The then 36-year-old Ronaldo fired in the goals as regularly as ever, but drama surrounded the star man from the start. Eventually, after an explosive interview with journalist Piers Morgan in November 2022, United moved on from their former saviour. Nonetheless, Ronaldo remains one of the club's greatest ever players.

WAYNE ROONEY
2004-2017

Born on the 24th of October 1985 in Croxteth, Liverpool, England, Wayne Mark Rooney made his debut for Manchester United on the 28th September 2004 against Fenerbahce. Rooney had scored a remarkable 99 goals in one season when he was spotted by an Everton Scout as a young schoolboy player. In his very first game for United, he scored a hat-trick in front of 67,000 at Old Trafford, and he was named Young Player of the Year at the end of the season.

Rooney's first trophy with United was the 2006 League Cup, and he also earned the title Man of the Match in that season when he scored twice against Wigan athletic in the League Cup final.

Nicknamed "Wazza", a name mirroring "Gazza", the nickname given to Paul Gascoigne the former England international, at the end of the 2006/07 season, he picked up his first Premier League winner's medal and became the youngest player in league history to reach 200 appearances on the 4th October 2008 in a game against Blackburn Rovers. Rooney ended that season with 20 goals in all competitions.

In 2009/10 Rooney became the PFA Players' Player of the Year and also became the FWA Footballer of the Year. That season was his most productive for the Red Devils when he scored 34 for goals before he was injured. He has won the BBC Match of the Day "Goal of the Season" award 3 times.

On the 21st of January 2017, Rooney finally beat Sir Bobby Charlton's record after scoring his 250th goal.

Apart from his prolific goal-scoring skills, Rooney, mostly used in a forward role but also as a midfielder, garnered praised for his versatility, pace, and movement off the ball. His conspicuously high work-rate and stamina were paired with dedication and the willingness to harry opponents and try to win back the ball and start counter-attacks.

With 253 goals to his credit, the most scored by any Manchester United player (Bobby Charlton scored 249), Rooney became one of the greatest players in the club's history, one of England's best players and all-time leading goalscorer.

Rooney left Manchester in 2017, moving to play for Everton the following season. He became manager of Derby County in 2020.

Wayne Rooney, who is also a boxer, married his long-term girlfriend, Coleen, (née McLoughlin), on the 12th of June 2008. They have four sons, Kai Wayne, 2009, Klay Anthony, 2013, Kit Joseph 2016 and Cass Mac, 2018.

WAYNE ROONEY'S AWARDS INCLUDE:

- Premier League Player of the Month, February 2005, December 2005, March 2006, October 2007, January 2010.
- England Senior Men's Player of the Year, 2008, 2009, 2014, 2015
- Premier League Goal of the Month, November 2017
- FWA tribute Award, 2017
- MLS Player of the Month, October 2018
- D.C United Golden Boot Winner, 2018

MICHAEL CARRICK

2006-2018

Michael Carrick was born on the 28th of July 1981 in Wallsend, Newcastle upon Tyne, England. He was five years old when his interest in football was awakened, and he started playing five-a-side games for Wallsend Boys Club, where his father was a volunteer. As a centre-forward, aged 12, he was selected for Burnside High School and then North Tyneside Schools. He was capped for the England Boys' club side.

He joined West Ham in 1997, the year he sat for his GCSE exams, staying with the club until 2004, often playing as a midfielder. This became his future role as he passed through Swindon Town, Birmingham City and Tottenham Hotspur on his way to Manchester United in 2006, where he was to play out the rest of his career, leaving in 2018. He played for the English national side from 2001 to 2015 and was the Manchester United Players' Player of the Year, 2012-13.

Carrick became coach for the Manchester United senior team in 2018.

Described as an "unassuming but highly intelligent and technically gifted deep-lying midfielder", Carrick was considered one of the best midfielders in Europe, who could read a game superbly well, influence the tempo and run of play in a game as well as creatively build attacking moves through his excellent crossing and passing skills.

Carrick married Lisa Roughead on the 16th of June 2007 and the couple have two children, daughter Louise and son Jacey.

MARCUS RASHFORD

2015 -

Marcus Rashford was born on the 31st of October 1997 in Manchester, England. The young Marcus would play football from an early age with his two brothers, Dane and Dwaine. In 1986 he was enrolled in a football centre, and his football life began as a goalkeeper for the Fletcher Moss Rangers. His dad was the coach. Even at the age of five, he was constantly kicking the ball at every opportunity, on a "different level" than the others boys, to quote David Horrocks of Fletcher Moss Rangers. Marcus's ambition paid dividends when he was seven; he was chosen to join the Manchester United Academy. At 12 years of age he was also the youngest to be accepted into their scholar's scheme and then the Youth Academy. Later, he studied with the Business and Technology Education Council and gained a National Diploma in Sports.

In 2012, he was included in the Manchester United U-15 squad, and later joined the English national U-16, U-18, U-20, and U-21 squads.

It was United manager David Moyes who agreed to Rashford's first professional contract, and the youngster joined the first team for the 2015-16 season making his debut in February 2016 in the UEFA Europa League scoring two goals. His Premier League debut came three days later; again he scored twice.

At the age of 18 years and 141 days, he became the youngest-ever scorer in the Premier League era Manchester derby.

Rashford became part of the England national team in 2016.

Rashford's early ambition continued into his professional career, his focus and dedication singling him out as potential captain material. He is always watching the best players in the world and ready to learn from them. His speed and reading of a game, his composure and spacial awareness coupled with his willingness to push opposition defenders and give them the slip them by finding space, using his dribbling skills to negotiate himself into positions when he can use his ferocious ability to score, have been praised many times.

Marcus Rashford has been extremely active in charity work and has been described as a "shining example" of somebody who is "passionate about community". He was made an MBE in 2020.

After a somewhat down year in a transitory period for the club in 2021/22, Rashford came back roaring under new boss Erik ten Hag. He was top scorer for the club with 30 goals in all competitions, including 17 in the Premier League - the best marks of the young attacker's career. Those goals led United to long-awaited silverware in the form of the Carabao Cup, scoring a goal in the final. He further embodied the main main role with winners against City and Liverpool and fantastic solo goals against Burnley and Wolves.

MARCUS RASHFORD'S AWARDS:

- Jimmy Murphy Young Player of the Year, 2015-16
- Premier League Player of the Month, January, 2019
- PFA Fan's Player of the Month, December, 2019
- Premier League Academy Graduate of the Year Award: 2019–20
- PFA Community Champion Award: 2019–20
- Manchester United Goal of the Season, 2019-20
- PFA Merit Award, 2020
- FIFA Foundation Award, 2020
- The Guardian Footballer of the Year, 2020
- FWA Tribute Award, 2020
- FIFAPro Merit Award, 2020
- Time 100 Next, 2021
- MBE, 2020
- Lockdown Heroes (Special Recognition), 2020 FSA Awards
- Expert Panel Special Award 2020 BBC Sports Personality of the Year

DAVID DE GEA QUINTANA

2011-2022

David de Gea Quintana was born on the 7th of November 1990 in Madrid, Spain.

Scouted at an early age by Atlético Madrid, de Gea made his first team debut for the club as goalkeeper in 2009 aged just 18. By 2011, his obvious talent meant that he was able to sign with Manchester United. He made his debut for the Spanish national side in 2014.

De Gea's unusual and elegant style of play, which involves making spectacular saves with his feet, is paired with superb athleticism and razor-sharp reflexes. He is thus equipped with a superb ability to prevent goals. He is also known for his composure and authority, which has often helped to turn a game.

Married to Edurne, a Spanish singer, the couple's first child, daughter Yanay, was born on the 4th of March 2021.

De Gea is considered to be one of the best goalkeepers in the world.

De Gea left United as a free agent in the summer of 2022 after a stellar 12 years as number 1, as Ten Hag led a rejuvenation of the squad to get the club back to former glory.

DAVID DE GEA'S AWARDS:

- PFA Fans' Premier League Player of the Month, November 2014.
- Sir Matt Busby Player of the Year, 2013-14, 2014-15, 2015-16, 2017-18
- Manchester United Players' Player of the Year: 2013–14, 2014–15, 2017–18
- Match of the Day Save of the Season: 2012–13, 2013–14, 2014–15, 2015–16, 2017–18
- Premier League Golden Glove, 2017-18, 2022-23

NEMANJA VIDIĆ

2006-2014

Nemanja Vidic was born on the 21st of October 1981 in Titovo Unice, SR Serbia, SFR Yugoslavia.

Vidic began playing football at the age of six, and by the age of twelve he was playing for Sloboda Unice. From there, he moved on to Red Star Belgrade, where he finished his youth career and played in his first team debut match in 2000.

His talent as a centre-back meant that in 2002 he was called up by the Serbian national team.

Following two years at Spartak Moscow, he signed for Manchester United in December 2005 making his debut on the 25th of January 2006. He stayed with the club until 2014, playing in 211 games before moving on to Internazionale, retiring in 2016.

Considered by many to be the world's best centre-back at the time, he combined strength and skill in the air with leadership qualities and spacial awareness. At Manchester, he and Rio Ferdinand formed a solid duo which was kernel of the United defence.

Vidic married Ana Ivanovic, a University of Belgrade economics student, on July the 17th in 2005. The couple have three sons, Luka, Stefan, and Petar.

NEMANJA VIDIĆ'S AWARDS:

- Premier League Player of the Season, 2008-09, 2010-11
- Premier League 20 Seasons Awards, 1992-93 to 2011-12
- Premier League Player of the Month, January 2009
- Sir Matt Busby Player of the Year, 2008, 2009
- Manchester United Players' Player of the Year, 2008-09
- Best Sportsman of SD Crvena Zvezda, 2020
- Serbia's Overseas Player of the Year, 2005 (Spartak Moscow), 2007, 2008, 2010 (Manchester United
- Serbian Footballer of the Year, 2005, 2008

PAUL POGBA

2016-2022

Paul Labile Pogba was born on the 15th of March 1993 in Lagny-sur-Marne France. Pogba has two brothers, Mathias and Florentin, and his parents separated in 1996 when he was two years old.

Paul attended school at Roissy-en-Brie and began playing football for the Union Sportiv Roissy-en-Brie team – a sport for which he soon developed a passionate interest. After seven years with the club, he successfully trialled for US Torcy in Seine-et-Marne and became captain on the U-13 squad.

His talent was noticed by professional club Le Havre, and one year after joining the team he was captain of the U-16 team and also called up to join the French national U-16 squad. Once again his ability brought him to the attention of talent scouts, and it was for Manchester United that he left France in 2009 to join the United Youth Academy, a move that gave rise to an acrimonious battle between the two clubs, which FIFA settled in United's favour.

Pogba moved from the Manchester U-18 side to the reserve squad one year later. He joined the United first team on the 19th of February 2011, but had to wait until the 31st of January 2012 for his debut.

Rumoured problems with United coach Alex Ferguson led to Pogba's decision to leave the club that year, and he moved to Juventus, where he grew to become a formidable player. One year later, in 2013, he became a member of the French national team. He stayed with the Italians until 2016, having acquired the nicknames "Il Polpo Paul" (Paul the Octopus) and "Pogboom", thanks to his bursts of volcanic energy.

In 2016, he rejoined United.

A strong midfielder, he is 6' 3" tall, Pogba works hard, is superb with balls in the air and possesses terrific stamina. In tandem with his dribbling ability, and accurate striking skills from well down the field, his leadership qualities and flair are unique and can turn the flow of a game in an instant.

Pogba is married to Maria Salaues Pogba, a Bolivian model and they have two children. Pogba was part of the World Cup winning team with France in 2018.

After 6 years and 154 appearances for United, Pogba returned to Juventus after a number of injury-riddled campaigns, hoping to regain his world-beating form.

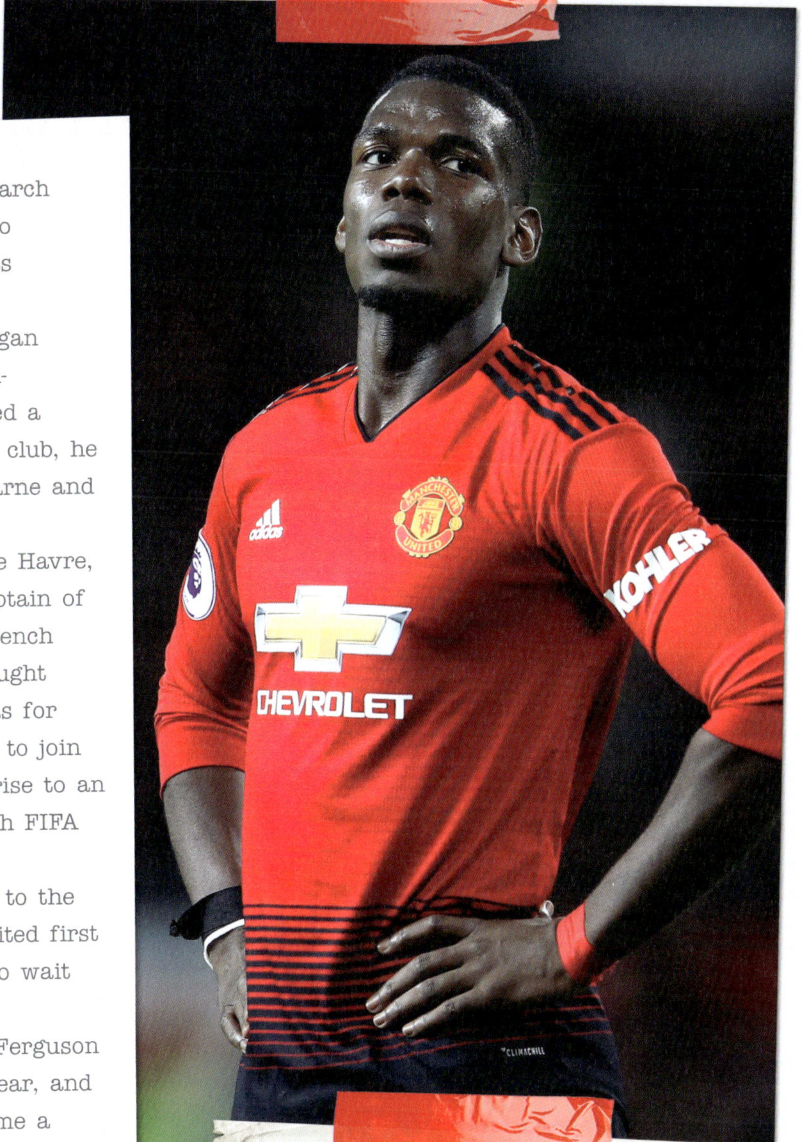

PAUL POGBA'S AWARDS INCLUDE:

- FIFA U-20 World Cup Golden Ball, 2013
- Golden Boy, 2013
- FIFA World Cup Best Young Player, 2014
- Bravo award, 2014
- UEFA Europa League Player of the Season, 2016–17
- World Cup winner's medal with France 2018
- Chevalier de la Légion d'Honneur, 2019

CARLOS HENRIQUE CASIMIRO 2022-

Carlos Henrique Casimiro, also known simply as Casemiro, was born on the 23rd of February 1992 in São José dos Campos, Brazil. Casemiro's talent was evident early on in his life and he was accepted into the São Paulo youth system, where his abilities saw him captain all of the squads from the age of 11.

His progression into the senior team came in 2010, and for the next three years, he made position of defensive midfielder his own. One year later, in 2011, he joined the Brazil senior squad. Once the European teams came knocking at his door, Casemiro departed for Spain and Real Madrid with whom he stayed until 2022.

Casemiro was already 30 years of age when Ten Hag came for him with an offer to move to the UK. He sent in a header for his first goal in the Premier League on 22nd of October 2022, made himself indispensable in his first season at the club and sealed his reputation by winning the award of the Alan Hardaker Trophy.

As befits a five-times Champions League winner, the 6' 1" Casemiro is armed with impressive physical and mental skills, speed that belies his tall frame, aggressive in his tackles, keen to intercept and adept at ruining opposition moves. His work rate is voracious and he is renowned for being able to steady and support his teammates up at the front, supplying them with intelligent passes to initiate offensive play. His reactions are sharp, his positional play spot on and he possess good technical abilities and a powerful shot. All this in tandem with great stamina and the ability to read the game and therefore anticipate play, help him to cordon off the defence as well as hold midfield. He has been nicknamed "the tank", which says it all.

BRUNO MIGUEL BORGES FERNANDES 2020-

Bruno Fernandes was born on the 8th of September 1994 in Maia, Portugal and began his professional career in 2002 with Portuguese club Infesta, moving on to Boavista two years later, where he remained until 2012. For the next five years, he played for three Italian sides, Novara, Udinese and Sampdoria, before returning to Portugal in 2017 to Sporting CP (also known as Sporting Lisbon). Having started out life as a centre-back, he eventually moved to an attacking midfielder position, where he has remained ever since.

By 2017, he had been called to play for the Portuguese U-19, U-20, U-21 and U-23 sides, at which point he joined the Portuguese national team. One year later he picked up the Primeira Liga Player of the Year award and developed into the highest-scoring midfielder in Portugal with 31 goals in the 2018/19 season. In the following season, he became only the third Sporting player in the 21st century to score in six or more consecutive appearances for the club.

Fernandes came to United in January of 2020, the season in which he scored 12 goals in total, and he hauled in the Premier League Player of the Month award four times that year. In his first full season of games in 2020/21, he put away an astonishing 28 goals. He also became top assist provider in the Champion's League.

Fernandes endeared himself to the fans when he commented sarcastically: "Dreams can't be (bought)", after the club had announced they would join a European Super League.

With a fierce work rate, 5' 10" Fernandes is not afraid to roam the pitch, finding space to attack, continuously vary the direction of his excellent passes, often high-risk through passes, and put away a huge array of goals. He will drop back to defend and then dictate the game's pace, and if called, take penalties with great success. All in all, one of the world's top midfielders.

Fernandes, who speaks fluent Spanish, English and Italian, married his childhood flame Ana Pinho in 2015. They have a daughter Matilde and a son Gonçalo.

BRUNO FERNANDES AWARDS INCLUDE:

- SJPF Young Player of the Month, August 2017, September 2017, October/November 2017, February 2018, April 2018
- Primeira Liga Goal of the Month, August 2017, September 2017
- Primeira Midfielder of the Month, August 2017 October/November 2018, December 2018, January 2019, February 2019, March 2019, April 2019, August 2019, September 2019
- Primeira Liga Player of the Month, August 2017, September 2017, April 2018, December 2018, February 2019, March 2019, April 2019
- Primeira Liga Player of the Year, 2017/18, 2018/19
- Sporting CP Footballer of the Year, 2018, 2019
- CNID Footballer of the Year, 2019
- PFA Fans' Premier League Player of the Month, February 2020
- UEFA Europa League Top Scorer, 2019/20
- Premier League Player of the Month, February 2020, June 2020, November 2020, December 2020
- Premier League Goal of the Month, June 2020, February 2021
- Sir Matt Busby Player of the Year, 2019/20, 2020/21
- Manchester United Goal of the Season, 2020/21
- FSA Men's Player of the Year Award, 2020

THE MANAGERS

A BRIEF LIST OF MANCHESTER UNITED MANAGERS

JAMES ERNEST MANGNALL

1903-1912

Born on 4th January 1866 at Bolton in Lancashire, England, he died on 13th January 1932.

Mangnall's contribution to the history of Manchester United was immense. He was the first manager to lead the team to trophy success and led the club from obscurity in Division Two into the mainstream of football. He also played a crucial role in moving the team to the Old Trafford stadium.

It took just three seasons for the new manager to see his club promoted to the First Division. He spent the money provided by businessman John Henry Davies wisely and made sure that his team worked on their physical fitness and the team spirit. In 1907/08 his work paid off and United took the First Division title and United won again in the 1910/11 season. Amidst controversy, Mangnall moved to Manchester City after the 1911/12 season.

The BUSBY YEARS

MATT BUSBY

1945 - 1969

Matt Busby was born in Scotland on 26th May 1909 and died on 20th January 1994. He was manager of Manchester United from 1945 until 1969 and again for a brief period in 1970/71.

Busby arrived at Manchester United after the Second World War without any managerial experience at the age of 36. He showed that he could be a tough disciplinarian with a ruthless streak beneath his friendly character. He hired Jimmy Murphy as chief coach and United finished the following three seasons in 2nd place and took the 1948 FA Cup.

By the start of the 1951 season Busby had put together an exciting team, which brought home the league championship title for the first time since 1911. Busby knew, however, that his team needed renewal and he began his policy of bringing in talented young players from the youth squad. This was the era of the "Busby Babes" and under Busby's tutelage such legendary names as Bobby Charlton, Duncan Edwards, and Dennis Viollet entered the senior team. Busby's decision paid off with two championships in 1956 and 1957.

In 1958, following a match against Red Star Belgrade the team's plane crashed killing 8 players and leaving Busby severely injured. The last rites were read to him twice but after 71 days he was well enough to return to Manchester.

Busby resumed full managerial responsibilities the following year and had to rebuild his team. Busby refused to alter his system and in the 1962/63 season United went to Wembley and won the FA Cup final against Leicester City.

In 1965 and 1967 United won the League championship again and in 1968 Busby realised his dream when United beat Benfica 4-1 at Wembley to win their first European Cup, the first English club to do so.

Busby retired in 1969 but remained at United for 11 years as a director before becoming club president in 1980. He was knighted for his services to football in 1968 the same year that he won Manager of the Year.

More than any other manager Busby sent his teams out to win but to play the game for pleasure not for war. It is thanks to him that Manchester United became known for exciting football full of showmanship, style and skill.

THOMAS HENDERSON "TOMMY" DOCHERTY

1971-1977

Born in Glasgow, Scotland on 24th April 1928. His first match in charge of Manchester United took place on 26th December 1972.

Docherty was the first manager of the post Busby era to stabilise United's position. Although he was unable to prevent United from being relegated, it took the club back up into the First Division the very next season and as a manager in the mould of Busby, his new young team went out to play attacking football and won the League championship in doing so.

Docherty led his team to play an attractive style of football that took them to the FA Cup final twice, lifting the cup at the second attempt by beating Liverpool.

Docherty seemed destined to bring United through a new era of success. Following an affair with the wife of the club's physiotherapist, he was sacked just 6 weeks after having won the cup. He had steered the club away from disaster and although his confident and often abrasive manner had also made him enemies, he remains a popular figure at United for having done so.

RON ATKINSON

1981-1986

Born on 18th March 1939 in Lancashire, England, he first took charge of a United match on 29th August 1981.

'Big Ron' Atkinson was an easy-going, extroverted character who brought about a revival of the team's fortunes but was unable to raise them higher in the league. By the end of his second season, United had won the FA Cup and although they showed inconsistency in form, they did win the FA Cup again in 1984/85. This lack of consistency in performance finally led to Atkinson's dismissal.

He went on to Sheffield Wednesday, Aston Villa and Coventry amongst others and is now a TV commentator.

ALEX FERGUSON

1986-2013

Born in Glasgow, Scotland on 31st December 1941, Ferguson attended Broomloan Road primary school and then Govan High School. He began his professional life as a forward for a variety of Scottish clubs, such as Rangers, the club he supported as a schoolboy, and Ayr United.

By 1974 he had turned to management, And ten years later was in charge of the Scottish National team.

He took charge of his first Manchester United match on the 8th of November 1986.

Alex Ferguson became one of the great managers in football history. He won 49 trophies with Manchester United presiding over the team during a period of extraordinary success. But when he arrived at the club, United were underachieving, unfit, and bedevilled by a culture of alcohol consumption.

Ferguson managed to revive the team but by the beginning of the 1989/90 season, it seemed that his job was on the line, as titles and trophies still evaded the team. The change came when United won the FA Cup in 1990.

Ferguson forged a powerful team and with Roy Keane and Eric Cantona he steered his club to their first "Double".

In the next ten seasons United picked up six more league titles and three FA Cup trophies but the year 1999 was the one that put Ferguson's name amongst the great managers. United won the "treble". That same year Ferguson was knighted for his achievements.

In 2008, he joined an elite group of managers who had won two Champions League titles.

Although he intended to retire at the end of the 2001/02 season, he decided to stay on as manager guiding his team to another league title in 2003. He finally led United to beat Liverpool's record of 18 league titles in 2011.

One year later on the 2nd of September 2012, Ferguson clocked up his 1,000th league game with United and just two weeks later, the 1-0 win over Galatasaray was his 100th Champions League victory.

Ferguson finally did retire in 2013 taking a position as UEFA Coaching Ambassador in 2014.

His record is astonishing; Ferguson has been awarded Manager of the Month more times than any other manager in British football history. He is the most successful British football manager in history with 49 trophies to his credit. He is also the only manager to win the Double north and south of the Scottish-English border and the only manager to bring his team into the first three places in the league in twenty consecutive seasons and win three consecutive titles, an achievement he repeated twice. He also claimed the English top division title thirteen times.

Valued for his vision and 'direct autocratic leadership style', Ferguson knew that long term success rather than short-term gain was the Holy Grail of coaching. Often thought of as aggressive and dominating and at other times as a father figure, he also was fiercely protective of his players, praising them, working with them on weak skills and instilling in them unconditional trust and confidence. But the excellence he expected of his players, he also expected of himself and his man-management skills were legendary. Losing was not an option; and as he said himself "I've never played for a draw in my entire life".

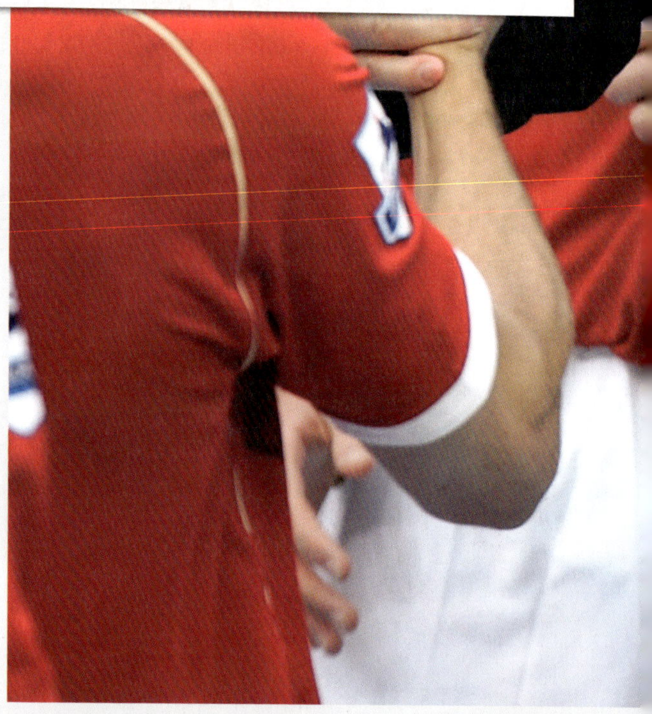

AMONGST A BEWILDERING ARRAY OF AWARDS AND DECORATIONS, FERGUSON HAS THESE INDIVIDUAL AWARDS:

- LMA Manager of the Decade for the 1990s.
- LMA Manager of the Year in 1998/99, 2007/08, 2010/11, 2012/13.
- Premier League Manager of the Season in 1993/94, 1995/96, 1996/97, 1998/99, 1999/2000, 2002/03, 2006/07, 2007/08, 2008/09, 2010/11, 2012/13.
- Premier League Manager of the Month, 27 times.
- IFFHS World's Best Club Coach in 1999 and 2008.
- BBC Sports Personality of the Year Coach Award for 1999.
- BBC Sports Personality of the Team of Year Award for 1999.
- BBC Sports Personality of the Year Lifetime Achievement Award for 2001.
- UEFA Manager of the Year for 1998/99.
- Onze d'Or Coach of the Year for 1999, 2007 and 2008.
- IFFHS World's Best Club Coach of the 21st Century in 2012.
- World Soccer Magazine Greatest Manager of all Time in 2013.
- BBC Sports Personality Diamond Award for 2013.
- English Football Hall of Fame in 2002.
- Scottish Football Hall of Fame in 2004.
- European Hall of Fame in 2008.

JOSÉ MÁRIO DOS SANTOS MOURINHO FÉLIX

2016-2018

José Mourinho was born on the 26th of January 1963 in Setúbal, Portugal. His father, Félix Mourinho, was goalkeeper for the Portuguese national team. The youngster received his first coaching lessons by observing his father's training methods. After leaving school, the young 5ft 9in (1.74m) José joined the Beleneses youth team but realised at the age of 23 that he did not possess enough power or speed to be truly effective on the field.

He then taught physical education for five years in a variety of schools.

In 1989, Mourinho married Matilde 'Tami' Faria, and they have two children; Matilde and José Mário.

In 1996 Mourinho went to FC Barcelona, where he began assisting players in analysing opposing teams and then became assistant to manager Louis van Gaal.

In September 2000, Mourinho was given his first permanent management role when he took over at Benfica. By January 2002 he had moved to Futebol Clube do Porto, known as FC Porto.

It was at Porto that Mourinho's distinctive coaching style became evident when his defenders and midfielders used their physical attacking talents to pressurise their opponents, who then either lost the ball or were forced into long, unreliable passes. The results were dramatic and proof of Mourinho's unique abilities.

The Portuguese had become a true leader and guide to his players. His knowledge of the game and attacking football is unparalleled, and he will defend his players to the hilt, rightly or wrongly.

In June 2004 Mourinho, began his legendary career at Chelsea.

He is certainly a strong-minded and charismatic character, and his relationship with the press has been tempestuous.

Despite their professional rivalry, Mourinho confessed to being a fan of Sir Alex Ferguson's, and away from the pitch the two are friends. The methods of the two men also show similarities which are part of their success stories. "The team'', said Mourinho, "is completely closed. Anything you say outside, there is no chance it will go inside. So the team is really strong and compact. We know what we want and how to achieve it on the pitch."

Mourinho suddenly left the club on the 20th of September 2007. He had been Chelsea's most successful manager since the club's foundation in 1905. Mourinho joined Internazionale in June 2008.

His tenure at Inter Milan, is considered by many to be a 'golden era', for the club and Mourinho's talents were recognised when he won the Panchina d'Oro, Coach of the Year award, in Italy for 2009/10.

Mourinho was apparently already considering the managership at Manchester United once Sir Alex Ferguson retired. On the 28th of May 2010, however, he joined Real Madrid.

Then came the announcement in June 2013 that Mourinho was returning to the Chelsea fold bringing in the League title in 2015.

Outside of football, Mourinho's charity work includes a youth project, where he uses football to bring together Palestinian and Israeli children. His quick mind is evident elsewhere, too, for he speaks six languages; English, French, Italian, Catalan, Spanish and Portuguese.

Mourinho fulfilled another of his dreams by joining Manchester United on the 27th of May 2016.

MOURINHO'S PERSONAL AWARDS:

- Onze d'or Coach of the Year: 2005, 2010
- FIFA Ballon d'or World Coach of the Year: 2010 (Mourinho auctioned this trophy and donated the proceeds to The Sir Bobby Robson Foundation and Breakthrough Breast Cancer, in memory of his early mentor, Sir Bobby Robson, who died aged 76 in 2009.)
- IFFHS World's Best Club Coach: 2004, 2005, 2010, 2012
- Primeira Liga Manager of the Year: 2002/03, 2003/04
- Premier League Manager of the Year: 2004/05, 2005/06
- Premier League Manager of the Month: November 2004, January 2005, March 2007
- Serie A Manager of the Year: 2008/9, 2009/10
- Albo Panchina d'Oro: 2009/10
- Miguel Muñoz Trophy: 2010/11, 2011/12
- UEFA Manager of the Year: 2002/03, 2003/04
- UEFA Team of the Year: 2003, 2004, 2005, 2010
- World Soccer Magazine World Manager of the Year: 2004, 2005, 2010
- LPFP Awards Best Portuguese Manager in Foreign Countries: 2008/09, 2009/10
- BBC Sports Personality of the Year Coach Award: 2005
- La Gazzetta dello Sport Man of the Year: 2010
- International Sports Press Association Best Manager in the World: 2010
- Prémio Prestígio Fernando Soromenho: 2012
- Officer of the Order of Infante Dom Henrique;
- Honoris causa – an honorary degree awarded by the Technical University of Lisbon for his achievements in football;
- Football Extravaganza's League of Legends
- Portuguese Coach of the Century, 2015.
- PFA Portuguese Manager of the Year, 2017.

OLE GUNNAR SOLSKJÆR

2018-2021

Ole Gunnar Solskjær was born on the 26th of February 1973 in Kristiansund, Møre og Romsda Norway. Ole's father, Øyvind, Solskjær was a champion Greco-Roman wrestler, and Ole also trained in the sport.

Between the ages of eight and ten, he followed in his father's footsteps and trained as a Greco-Roman wrestler. He persevered for three years before his parents decided that his small frame was not suited to the rough and tumble of the sport and he should stop. Meanwhile, he'd become fascinated by football whilst watching British football games on television and eventually acquired a deep knowledge about the British game. The young Ole was a Liverpool fan, and when he was seven years old, he joined local 3rd Division football club Clausenengen.

In 1990, Solskjaer made his debut for the Clausenengen first team. He was then 17 years old, but had to fit in one year of national service in the Norwegian Army between 1992 and 1993. He would stay with Clausenengen for five years as a forward; he scored 115 goals in 109 games.

From 1994 to 1996, he played for 1st Division team Molde, before the 5'10" striker became a surprise acquisition by Alex Ferguson at Manchester United, playing his first full game in September. He remained with Manchester for the rest of his playing career, moving into management in 2008 at the Manchester United Academy, taking over the reserves in the summer of 2008.

There followed a period of coaching at Cardiff City sandwiched between two terms with his former club Molde, the first in 2011, the second in 2015, whereupon he returned to United as their first team manager in 2018.

When questioned about his management style, Solskjaer has commented that: "There are different ways to motivate and inspire players, and I do not always believe in scaring them to play better... I like my behaviour, my personality and my values. I stand by them. It also works closely with the players, the dialogue is good... Sometimes you are tough, sometimes you give players a pat on the shoulder."

Solskjaer has named Pep Guardiola as his role model, and the Catalan's methods are detectable in Solskjaer's desire for attacking play; he also wants his defenders to be proactive, winning the ball back quickly. It's from the back that Solskjaer will build an attack, creating central space by using maximum width. Against the top teams, his preferred formation will be a 5-3-2, and normally 4-2-3-1.

Solskjær's training sessions have been described as "innovative", and he is certainly prepared to escape from rigid thinking, whilst possessing a clear vision of how his team should perform.

After a number of seasons of falling just short of the top honours, Solksjaer left the club in November 2021 after embarrassing defeats to rivals Liverpool, 5-0, City 2-0 and lowly Watford 4-1. The club appointed interim Ralf Rangnick to steady the ship, before choosing Erik Ten Hag for the permanent job.

OLE GUNNAR SOLSKJÆR'S AWARDS:

- Knight of the order of St. Olav, First Class, 2008
- Kniksen Awards:
- Kniksen of the Year, 1996
- Kniksen's Honour Award, 2007
- Coach of the Year, 2011, 2012
- Peer Gynt Prize, 2009 (for football and philanthropy)
- Premier League Manager of the Month, January 2019

ERIK TEN HAG

2022-

Erik ten Hag was born on 2nd of February 1970 in Haaksbergen Netherlands.

His playing career began as centre-back in 1989 with Dutch team Twente, and he continued his career, always playing for teams in the Netherlands, returning to Twente in 1992 until 1994 and again in 1996 until 2002, when he ended his playing career.

Ten Hag's managerial career began 10 years later in 2012 when he spent a year with Dutch team Go Ahead Eagles, before moving to coach Bayern Munich, in 2013, where he stayed for the next two years. He then moved to Dutch club Utrecht and followed that job by becoming head coach of Ajax with whom he won the Eredivisie - the highest level of professional football in the Netherlands - in 2018/19, 2020/21 and 2021/22, the KNVB Cup in 2018/19 and 2020/21 and the Johan Cruyff Shield in 2019.

Considered a rising managerial star, his call to join United came on the heels of a very disappointing year for the Manchester club, and he was given a contract until June 2025. After two losses in the 2022/23 season, Ten Hag assembled a team that could go toe-to-toe with the best in the Premier League. In doing so, he became the first Manchester United manager to reach 20 competitive wins in the fastest time frame, 27 games.

The manager readily admits that Pep Guardiola influenced his game plans - Guardiola's desire to play an attractive and attacking game - while he was at Bayern Munich, and he employs that attacking mentality himself, thus freeing his strikers to achieve their best performances. He is also known to employ Total Football, a Dutch concept of triangles to overload vital areas of the pitch on and off the ball. This opens up possibilities for players in various areas and releases them to roam around the pitch. He will also assist his favourite players, enabling them to unfold and develop their talents in the best way.

Erik ten Hag and his wife, Bianca, have a son and two daughters, and he won the Rinus Michels Award for 2015/16, 2018/19, 2020/21, and the Premier League, Manager of the Month for September 2022 and February 2023.

THE STATISTICS

POSITION IN THE LEAGUE:

DIVISION TWO

1902/03 - 5
1903/04 - 3
1904/05 - 3
1905/06 - 2

DIVISION ONE

1906/07 - 8
1907/08 - 1
1908/09 - 13
1909/10 - 5
1910/11 - 1
1911/12 - 13
1912/13 - 4
1913/14 - 14
1914/15 - 18

WORLD WAR I

1919/20 - 12
1920/21 - 13
1921/22 - 22

DIVISION TWO

1922/23 - 4
1923/24 - 14
1924/25 - 2
1925/26 - 9
1926/27 - 15
1927/28 - 18
1928/29 - 12
1929/30 - 17
1930/31 - 22

DIVISION TWO

1931/32 - 12
1932/33 - 6
1933/34 - 20
Division Two
1934/35 - 5
1935/36 - 1

DIVISION ONE

1936/37 - 21

DIVISION TWO

1937/38 - 2

DIVISION ONE

1938/39 - 14

WORLD WAR II

1946/47 - 2
1947/48 - 2
1948/49 - 2
1949/50 - 4
1950/51 - 2
1951/52 - 1
1952/53 - 8
1953/54 - 4
1954/55 - 5
1955/56 - 1
1956/57 - 1
1957/58 - 9
1958/59 - 2
1959/60 - 7
1960/61 - 7
1961/62 - 15
1962/63 - 19
1963/64 - 2
1964/65 - 1

1965/66 – 4
1966/67 – 1
1967/68 – 2
1968/69 – 11
1969/70 – 8
1970/71 – 8
1971/72 – 8
1972/73 – 18
1973/74 – 21

DIVISION TWO

1974/75 – 1

DIVISION ONE

1975/76 – 3
1976/77 – 6
1977/78 – 10
1978/79 – 9
1979/80 – 2
1980/81 – 8
1981/82 – 3
1982/83 – 3
1983/84 – 4
1984/85 – 4
1985/86 – 4
1986/87 – 11
1987/88 – 2
1988/89 – 11
1989/90 – 13
1990/91 – 6
1991/92 – 2

PREMIERSHIP

1992/93 – 1
1993/94 – 1
1994/95 – 2
1995/96 – 1
1996/97 – 1
1997/98 – 2
1998/99 – 1
1999/2000 – 1
2000/01 – 1
2001/02 – 3
2002/03 – 1
2003/04 – 3
2004/05 – 3
2005/06 – 2
2006/07 – 1
2007/08 – 1
2008/09 – 1
2009/10 – 2
2010/11 – 1
2011/12 – 2
2012/13 – 1
2013/14 – 7
2014/15 – 4
2015/16 – 5
2016/17 – 6
2017/18 – 2
2018/19 – 6
2019/20 – 3
2020/21 – 2
2020/21 – 2
2021/22 – 6
2022/23 – 3

MORE STATS

CUP COMPETITIONS:

FA CUP

1908/09 – Man United 1-0 Bristol City
1947/48 – Man United 4-2 Blackpool
1956/57 – Man United 1-2 Aston Villa
1957/58 – Man United 0-2 Bolton Wanderers
1962/63 – Man United 3-1 Leicester
1975/76 – Man United 0-1 Southampton
1976/77 – Man United 2-1 Liverpool
1978/79 – Man United 2-3 Arsenal
1982/83 – Man United 2-2 Brighton and Hove Albion
1982/83 – Man United 4-0 Brighton and Hove Albion
1984/85 – Man United 1-0 Everton
1989/90 – Man United 3-3 Crystal Palace
1993/94 – Man United 4-0 Chelsea
1994/95 – Man United 0-1 Everton
1995/96 – Man United 1-0 Liverpool
1998/99 – Man United 2-0 Newcastle United
2003/04 – Man United 3-0 Millwall
2004/05 – Man United 0-0 Arsenal (U.L.O.P 4-5)
2006/07 – Man United 0-1 Chelsea
2015/16 – Man United 2-1 Crystal Palace

THE LEAGUE CUP

1982/83 – Man United 1-2 Liverpool
1990/91 – Man United 0-1 Sheffield Wednesday
1991/92 – Man United 1-0 Nottingham Forest
1993/94 – Man United 1-3 Aston Villa
2002/03 – Man United 0-2 Liverpool
2005/06 – Man United 4-0 Wigan Athletic
2008/09 – Man United 0-0 Tott. Hotspur (U.W.O.P 4-1)
2009/10 – Man United 2-1 Aston Villa

EUROPEAN CUP / CHAMPIONS LEAGUE

1967/68 – Man United 4-1 Benfica
1998/99 – Man United 2-1 Bayern Munich
2007/08 – Man United 1-1 Chelsea (U.W.O.P 6-5)
2008/09 – Man United 0-2 Barcelona
2010/11 – Man United 1-3 Barcelona

FA COMMUNITY SHIELD

1908 – Man United 1-1 QPR
1908 – Man United 4-0 QPR (replay)
1911 – Man United 8-4 Swindon Town
1948 – Man United 4-3 Arsenal
1952 – Man United 4-2 Newcastle United
1956 – Man United 1-0 Manchester city
1957 – Man United 4-0 Aston Villa
1963 – Man United 0-4 Everton
1965 – Man United 2-2 Liverpool (shared)
1967 – Man United 3-3 Tottenham Hotspur (shared)
1977 – Man United 0-0 Liverpool (shared)
1983 – Man United 2-0 Liverpool
1985 – Man United 0-2 Everton
1990 – Man United 1-1 Liverpool (shared)
1993 – Man United 1-1 Arsenal (U.W.O.P 5-4)
1994 – Man United 2-0 Blackburn Rovers
1996 – Man United 4-0 Newcastle United
1997 – Man United 1-1 Chelsea (U.W.O.P 4-2)

1998 – Man United 0-3 Arsenal
1999 – Man United 1-2 Arsenal
2000 – Man United 0-2 Chelsea
2001 – Man United 1-2 Liverpool
2003 – Man United 1-1 Arsenal (U.W.O.P 4-3)
2004 – Man United 1-3 Arsenal
2007 – Man United 1-1 Chelsea (U.W.O.P 3-0)
2008 – Man United 0-0 Portsmouth (U.W.O.P 3-0)
2009 – Man United 2-2 Chelsea (U.L.O.P 4-1)
2010 – Man United 3-1 Chelsea
2011 – Man United 2-3 Manchester City
2013 – Man United 2-0 Wigan Athletic
2016 – Man United 2-1 Leicester City

EUROPEAN CUP-WINNERS' CUP

1990/91 – Man United 2-1 Barcelona

EUROPEAN SUPER CUP

1991/92 – Man United 1-0 Red Star Belgrade
1999/2000 – Man United 0-1 Lazio
2008/09 – Man United 1-2 Zenit St. Petersburg

FIFA CLUB WORLD CUP/INTERCONTINENTAL CUP

1968/69 – 1st leg Man United 0-1 Estudiantes
2nd Leg Man United 1-1 Estudiantes

INTERCONTINENTAL CUP

1999 – Man United 1-0 Palmeiras

CLUB WORLD CUP

2008 – Man United 1-0 Liga de Quito

EFL CUP

2106/017 – Man United 3-2 Southampton
2016/17 – Man United 3-2 Southampton
2022/23 – Man United 2-0 Newcastle United

UEFA EUROPA CUP

2017 – Man United 2-0 Ajax

A.S. MONACO
MANCHESTER UNITED F.C.
STADE LOUIS II - MONACO
036 AS MONACO
UEFA CHAMPIONS LEAGUE QF2
WED 18/03/98 KICK OFF 7:45PM
North Stand Tier 1 Upper
BARCLAYS PREMIER LEAGUE
LIVERPOOL V MANCHESTER UNIT
Sunday 1st September 2013
KICKOFF 1.30PM
ANFIELD ROAD LOWER
TURNSTILE:N 1-2
LIVERPOOL FOOTBALL CLUB
FC Bayern München
Manchester United FC
Mittwoch, 9. April 2014 20:45 Uhr
Allianz Arena München
Challenge Cup Competition
FINAL TIE
REPLAY
FINAL UEFA CHAMPIONS LEAGUE'99
ESTADI FC BARCELONA, 26 MAY 1999, 20:45
EUROPA LEAGUE
UEFA.com
RESPECT
Stadium Feijenoord
BUDP
Date :15-9-2016
Time :19:00
Open :17:30
Price :206,70 EURO
FEYENOORD -
MANCHESTER UNITED
LEAGUE MATCH
Manchester Utd. v. Chelsea
WEDNESDAY, 23rd AUGUST, 1961
FINAL
MOSCOW 2008
MANCHESTER UNITED F.C. PLC
OLD TRAFFORD, MANCHESTER
EUROPEAN CUP WINNERS CUP COMPETITION
QUARTER FINAL TIE — 2nd LEG
MANCHESTER UNITED
v.
F.C. BARCELONA
WEDNESDAY, 21st March, 1984
Kick-off 7-30 p.m.
PADDOCK
ADMISSION
£2.10
West Ham United F.C.
WEST HAM UNITED
versus
MANCHESTER UTD
FINAL TIE
SATURDAY, MAY 4th, 1963
KICK-OFF 3 p.m.
EMPIRE STADIUM, WEMBLEY
The Football Association Cup Competition
2006
CARLING CUP
FINAL 2006
MILLENNIUM STADIUM, CARDIFF
Sunday 26 Feb, 2006
KICK OFF 15:00 GATES OPEN 13:00
GATE 6 ENTRY A1
BLOCK L22 ROW 17 AISLE 322
MANCHESTER UNITED F.C. SEAT 5
MAN UTD AREA
£36.00
The FA CUP FINAL
ARSENAL V MANCHESTER UTD
KICK OFF 15:00 GATES OPEN 13:00
GATE 6 ENTRY A1 AISLE 318
BLOCK L18 ROW 13 SEAT 6
MANCHESTER FA
£ 65.00
MAN UTD AREA
WEMBLEY
Football Association Challenge Cup
SAT., 18 MAY
THE FA CUP SPONSORED BY E.ON
CHELSEA V
MANCHESTER UNITED
19 MAY 2007
ENTRANCES OPEN 12 NOON
OPENING CEREMONY FROM 1:30 PM
KICK OFF 3:00 PM
ENTRANCE E
BLOCK 506
FIRST DIVISION LEAGUE MATCH
MANCHESTER UTD.
v
LIVERPOOL
SEMI-FINAL
Saturday, 16th April, 1983
Manchester United
v.
Arsenal
Kick-off 3.00 p.m.
PRICE
£3.00
Incl. V.A.T.
MANCHESTER UTD. F.C. LTD.
OLD TRAFFORD, MANCHESTER
EUROPEAN CHAMPIONS CLUB CUP
Semi Final—2nd Leg
MANCHESTER UNITED
v
A.C. MILAN (ITALY)
DATE AS ANNOUNCED
Kick-off 7-45 p.m.
Reserved Seat 30/-
STAND
H
Reserved Wing
STAIRWAY
11
Turn Left
Audi Cup
Bayern München
Boca Juniors
THE FA COMMUNITY SHIELD
7 AUGUST 2016
SATURDAY 21 MAY 2016
KICK OFF 17:30